MW00780375

"I used to get so frustrated wit ready to quit. It was so clear after our Windows why I wasn't able to relate effectively. Once I started speaking to my boss from her Window, our relationship changed dramatically. Within two months, I received a $5000 bonus!"

J.U.
Director
Verizon Communications

"Bottom line, this training helps every single individual to become a better person on both a personal and professional level."

Boyce Morrow

"Understanding my Window and others that I work with changed my relationships 180 degrees! I had no idea how I was coming across to my boss and co-workers. Before, I would get very frustrated and judgmental, oftentimes pointing at them at being the problem. By making small changes in my way of communicating that aligned with their respective Windows, I was able to create win-wins in my relationships."

M.B.
Senior Client Manager
Wells Fargo Corporation

"In my thirty-five plus years in the training profession, this is by far the most usable model I've found. In fact, quite a few leaders in my company who didn't initially plan to attend the workshop, upon hearing others describe its value, requested to attend. This has been a huge success, and we expect dividends reaching far into the future."

Jeff Gossett
Founder
Tailwinds Consulting

Everyone Is a Jerk to Someone, Every Day

Painless Ways to Improve
Communication with Individuals and Teams

Rebecca M. Rhodes

Published by the Institute of Leadership Development, 2734 Calvary Ct., Fort Mill, SC 29715.

Published in association with ARC Publishing, 3775 EP True Parkway, Suite 217, West Des Moines, IA 50265.

Cover and inside design by Maria Ines Comparini.

Cover image from Mega Pixels / Shutterstock.com
Image used under license from Shutterstock.com
Inside images from PresenterMedia. Used by permission. All rights reserved.

First edition

ISBN: 978-0-6926-7457-4

DEDICATION

I dedicate this book first to my son, Christian, for his gentle pushing that it was time to write. Secondly, I dedicate this to all those who keep asking for more about the Time Communication Model when I teach it. May it be a blessing and a resource.

ACKNOWLEDGMENTS

How do I say thanks to all those who have been a part of my learning, growing, and getting to the place I am today. . . .

In writing this book, I thank those who pushed me to get it going—my friends at the Global Celebration School of Supernatural Ministry and my son, Christian. Simultaneously, they insisted it was time, and they were right!

The teams at FamilyArc and ARC Centers have been incredible to work with in designing and editing. Juan, Ruthie, Missy, Maria, Laurie—you guys are the greatest.

My team at ILD, thank you: Natalie, Nils, Shane, Justin, and Jody, for editing and helping me get it done. Rhonda and Eric, for modeling the material in every aspect of your lives, both personally and professionally. And to Richard Blumhagen, the best business partner ever for over twelve years, as we applied the principles of this Model in everything we did.

CONTENTS

Preface

Who have you been a jerk to today?

I'm going to assume that you didn't wake up this morning planning to be a jerk. However, you will most likely do or say something today that will cause a misunderstanding, and someone will walk away perceiving you as just that.

In my thirty years of coaching individuals and teams on improving communication, I have found that we often judge ourselves by our intentions and others by their actions. The key to good communication is being able to recognize that we're all perceiving things differently. Nine times out of ten, misunderstandings can be avoided if we take the time to clarify our meanings and seek to understand where each person is coming from.

In *Everyone Is a Jerk to Someone, Every Day*, we'll take a closer look at the different perceptions of time and communication in order to improve understanding and reduce frustration with every person in your environment.

Introduction

The subject of communication has always fascinated me. Why? Because throughout my life I have felt misunderstood. So as I began my journey of living "on purpose," the study of communication became a big part of that experience.

Do you remember any life-changing events for yourself? I remember several of them, but the most profound occurred in 1980 when I reluctantly agreed to attend a class on time management. As a training manager for a commercial bank, I was always looking for material to teach that would benefit the employees and the organization. Time management was a subject I personally liked to avoid because it seemed too difficult actually to do. One persistent salesman wore my resistance down, however, and I signed up to attend his two-day class. Little did I know the profound impact those two days would have on me, both then and throughout the rest of my life.

In that class, the persistent salesman, John E. Davies, taught us about a simple-to-understand-and-apply model about people's perceptions of time. That model opened my eyes to the idea of looking beyond "managing time" to understanding human behavior and, more especially, to understanding myself.

This is my story of how those two days have continued to impact me and everyone I have come in contact with in the thirty-four years since then. I call it my "story" because I have learned I am a story collector, and I believe we can learn lessons with less offense through stories as opposed to someone just telling us a truth.

At the time that I took the time management class from him, John owned a company called Identity Dimensions in Kissimmee, Florida. He developed a tool that he called DATUM (Dimensional Analysis of Time Use Motivation). When I first met him, he was using DATUM to teach time management and was working on developing materials to teach communication and presentation skills. We lost contact for a period of time, but when I settled in North Carolina and was working in another bank, I contacted him about using the material. To my surprise, I learned he had sold the company to a group called AHP Systems. They had put his materials in a warehouse with no intention of using them, so when I asked them about the materials in 1985, they sold me the rights to use them for $1.00.

Since that time, I have developed John's concepts into what I call the Time Communication Model. This is the foundational tool we use in my company, the Institute of Leadership Development (ILD). Founded in 1989, ILD is a coaching, training, and consulting company that works with organizations, ministries, businesses, and individuals to build better leaders through emphasizing strong communication skills.

As I considered how to write this story, I found it interesting to see how the very concepts I wanted to write about began to influence my thoughts, feelings, and actions. The Time Communication Model is all about perception, and Davies used time as the common point to help all of us understand how our brains process information.

Writing this book caused me to assume my usual stance of procrastination and lack of confidence. I decided to read a book entitled *How to Write a Lot: A Practical Guide to Productive Academic Writing* by Paul J. Silvia. The main premise of the book is that it takes a commitment of *time* to write a lot. Anyone who wasn't willing to commit at least four hours a week to write should forget about it and give his book to someone else.

"Wow," I thought, "I can give four hours a week," and I promptly scheduled writing times on my calendar.

But then the second time I was scheduled to write, I overslept and began the day under time pressure. According to Davies' research, time pressure takes a person out of their relaxed state of mind. Personally, I have found that I am most creative when I am in a relaxed state of mind. I was extremely unproductive that day, but it became a perfect example of how perceptions and time drive us to react and respond. When I stopped giving control to time and took a breath, clarity and creativity returned. Time is flexible, I realized. I don't have to live by the clock. If time isn't where I need it to be, I can re-arrange my schedule. After all, four hours out of 168 hours in a week is nothing.

It was my old definition of time that drove me to react to oversleeping and to put myself under time pressure in the first place. Once I understood that, I had the ability to change it. This is another important truth about perceptions—they can be changed!

The definition of perception that best speaks to me about understanding the Time Communication Model comes from Webster's 1972 New World Dictionary of the American Language.

Perception: Mental grasp of objects, qualities, etc., by means of the senses

Our brains process data in four different ways to bring clarity and understanding. Although all four processes exist in each brain, the strength of each process is determined by two factors: what we were born with (genetic) and what we have learned (life experience). It is those differences in processes that cause us to have different perceptions, which then drive misunderstandings in communication.

Simple, but complex at the same time, isn't it?

So, in the event that you are reading this book and haven't taken the Time Communication Analysis or attended a "Welcome to My Windows" class before, let me explain the Model for you.

Your brain processes the data received from your five senses (taste, touch, smell, sight, hearing), and as the data enters, it is filtered through the four perception processes.

The first two are genetic and determine how we view our world: through a *focused* perception or a *diffused* perception (how intense each of these perceptions is in us has already been determined at birth). Even though we can learn to use them both, the perception that was stronger at birth will remain a preference and can be defined as our default setting. People who use the focused perception process tend to see what's directly in front of them. They can be very intense and unaware of other things, spending long periods of time looking at or working on one thing. People who use the diffused perception process, on the other hand, are aware of what is directly in front of them but can also immediately turn their attention to other things going on around them. They are sometimes described as easily distracted and always moving.

GENETIC PERCEPTIONS

FOCUSED   DIFFUSED

The other two perception processes come from life experience and are learned. They determine how we view individual events in our lives. Some of us walk through life experiencing each event separately without looking for any connections to other events. This is called a discontinuous view. Others of us prefer to connect each event to another one in order to gain understanding. We call this a continuous view.

LIFE EXPERIENCE PERCEPTIONS

DISCONTINUOUS
SPATIAL TIME

CONTINUOUS
LINEAR TIME

When you put the four lenses together, it looks like this (forming a window):

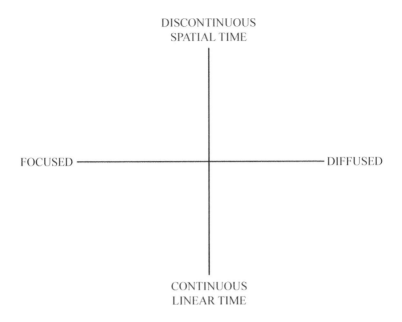

The Way We View Our World

The combination of the processes leads us to view our world through those perceptions and causes us to view everything through a particular time frame. All of this will be discussed further in later chapters.

John Davies gave each Window a name:

    Focused/Discontinuous – Producer – Present Time Frame

    Discontinuous/Diffused – Imaginist – Future Time Frame

    Diffused/Continuous – Teamist – Past Time Frame

    Continuous/Focused – Analyst – Past, Present, and Future Time Frames in equal proportions

So the Model looks like this:

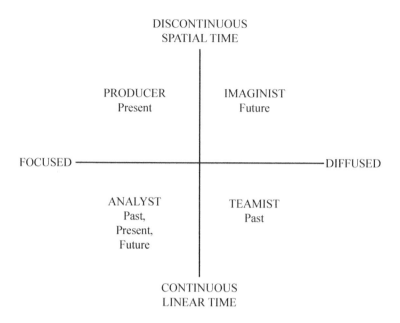

DISCONTINUOUS
SPATIAL TIME

PRODUCER
Present

IMAGINIST
Future

FOCUSED ——————————————————————— DIFFUSED

ANALYST
Past,
Present,
Future

TEAMIST
Past

CONTINUOUS
LINEAR TIME

Intensities of the Numbers Can Bring Confusion and Understanding

The Time Communication Analysis is an eighteen-question instrument that measures the intensity of each of your perception processes into the four Window panes. It shows the intensity of each Window in two ways: in your relaxed state and under the pressure of time. Each Window is scored on a scale of 0-45 points. The higher the score, the stronger a person operates in that Window. To take the Analysis or to learn more visit, you can visit ILD's website: www.ileadershipdevelopment.com.

Let's talk for a minute about the importance of intensities. Any time the number in a Window falls between 0-12, it implies that a person will reject that Window and the time frame associated with it. I have a 12 in the Analyst Window. I do not like to utilize these perception processes or to spend time using that particular mindset—one which represents structure, order, correctness, and attention to detail. I can get there, but to stay there for very long gives me a headache. That means detailed work is boring for me, and doing things like expense reports, written reports, etc. are tasks I would prefer to avoid.

If the number in the Window falls between 13-17, that person will avoid the Window and associated time frame whenever possible. I have a 13 in the Producer Window. I do not do things just to keep busy. I need to have a purpose behind a task, or I am not likely to get it done. Again, I can go there, but it takes effort.

If the number in the Window falls between 18-22, a person will tolerate that Window and associated time frame. He flows in and out of it fairly easily without being under duress while doing it. For example, a person with a 19 Teamist can tolerate being around others but needs frequent breaks from them to recoup energy. They enjoy moments of solitude or working alone.

If the number falls between 23-29, a person is well-developed in that Window and in the associated time frame. It is comfortable and natural, and she likes living and communicating through it. I know a person with a 29 Producer. He constantly needs to be busy with a to-do list full of varying activities; otherwise, he feels as if he is wasting time.

When a number reaches an intensity of 30 or higher, a person is over-developed in that Window and the associated time frame. This is not necessarily negative; it just means that this person's preference is so strong that it will be highly visible to others, and if it is not compatible to someone else's preferred Window, this might become a source of irritation or frustration in their relationship. I met a man once who had a Teamist score of 34. He had spent twenty-plus years working alone in a wood yard driving a crane. People called him mean. What he learned from taking this instrument was that he was miserable working alone. Once he started a new job where he could interact regularly with people, his whole demeanor changed, and no one called him "mean" again.

Your thought process is generally set somewhere around age twenty-two to twenty-four, and it will not change readily more than five points for the remainder of your life. The only time I have seen someone's scores change is after an extreme life trauma, or when they were not honest the first time they took the assessment.

Paying attention to these intensities in yourself and in others brings clarity to relationships, communication, and differences in behavior. The confusion starts to go away once you recognize that, most of the time, the person you are having difficulty working or communicating with generally works through one of your weaker Windows. Your perceptions are sometimes polar opposites, resulting in occasional confusion or hurt feelings.

Subtle Differences Can Cause "Pain" in the Panes

The next step in understanding your Windows or someone else's is to recognize how the numbers work together. If your highest Window is ten points higher than their scores in any of the others, you will tend to see purely from that Window's perspective, with little influence from other Windows. This is not painful to your communication process with someone who is in the same Window as you (except for another Producer who might battle for control). But an especially high score in a single Window can become very painful when communicating with someone in an opposite Window, especially when that Window is your highest and their lowest, or their highest and your lowest.

If your top two Windows are within 6-9 points of each other, you tend to process through the higher Window most of the time, but occasionally, the other Window begins to influence your thinking.

I find that most people who have studied this material focus on the highest Window of the person they are communicating with, and then they become confused when that person begins to show signs of behaviors from his or her secondary Window. When I coach people about this, it takes practice for them to look for, and include, the necessary information for the second Window in their communication with the other person.

When two Windows are within five points of each other (0-5), it becomes more difficult to determine exactly which Window the person is working from. This is because he tends to run back and forth between Windows at will (similar to a "Square," discussed in Chapter 7), and it can be difficult to pinpoint him between the two (or sometimes three) Windows. If you have two similar scores like this, you may notice confusion or pain while trying to understand your waffling.

The pain alluded to in this section is a result of the fact that the slight differences in numbers can significantly impact how a person thinks or hears and cause you frustration when trying to make sure that person understands your message. A Producer/Teamist does not hear the same way a Teamist/Producer hears, and if you ignore the difference, you may emphasize the wrong information or misread the message sent back to you.

So it can get complicated, because you have to think both about their differences and about your own. To forget either one can lead to great pain in your relationship.

I have a client now who is a Teamist/Imaginist. Everyone who works with him sees the Imaginist because it is quite strong, especially under pressure of time. Since that is where they see him most of the time, they ignore his Teamist side when communicating with him and then are frustrated by his reactions. I continuously have to remind them not to forget his Teamist side. He hears through that Window first.

One last thought before we get started. It is so natural for us to filter what we are reading and want to apply it to ourselves. Be self-aware and try to avoid judging, comparing, or applying every situation I discuss in this book to yourself. Anytime we attempt to become something we are not, we subject ourselves to extreme stress, which can cause physical, emotional, and mental repercussions over time.

In order to gain the most benefit from reading this book, I ask that you be open and not allow your beliefs to thwart new ideas. Let your mind ponder the possibilities, and listen to your inner-self for personal truths.

Chapter 1
It's Not All About Me

Can you remember when you first grasped the reality that it wasn't all about you? I cannot remember when this happened for me, but I am reminded of this reality almost daily. As I was writing this book, several great examples of this have happened.

The first reminder of this reality happened on a FaceTime call with a client who was trying to understand the communication style differences between other Windows and her own High Teamist viewpoint.

"Why are Imaginists so mean?" she asked.

As you learn more about me, you will come to understand that, as an Imaginist/Teamist (with Window scores that are only one point apart), that statement led me to react with the question, "Am I mean?" It is what we do as Imaginists/Teamists. As the Imaginist, I have the propensity to take something someone says and see all of the negative implications. As the Teamist, I took what was said and made it personal to me.

I shared this with my client, and after sharing a great laugh over my Imaginist/Teamist response, I explained that her question was a perfect "Teamist" question. It is natural for a strong Teamist, like her, to perceive others' actions and words often as "mean," and then I helped her to understand why that was true.

The second reminder that it was not all about me came at a family gathering where we were all reminiscing about our childhoods. One story I related was about the time that my family was moving, and my father decided to go hunting in spite of the scheduled move. My mother was so angry at him that she moved out while he was gone and left a note on the front door of our old home saying, "Find us if you can."

My sister-in-law turned to me at the end of my recounting the story. "All these years I thought she did that to get away from me," she said.

"No, it was all aimed at our father, not you," I replied.

All those years, she had been carrying that hurt because of her perception, which turned out to be a total misunderstanding.

The third incident occurred at the same family gathering. Other family members started recounting how I was our mother's "favorite" and how very spoiled they all thought I was. My perception of my childhood, on the other hand, was that our oldest brother was the favorite and that I was totally rejected by my mom until I turned fifteen and even then she only wanted to control my life.

Who was right, and who was wrong? No one! It's all about different perceptions. No matter what I see, hear, feel, think, or do, I process it through my perception filters, which makes me think it's all about me.

So what does this have to do with communication? Well, every day, we communicate to others. Sometimes it involves words, but often our actions and behaviors speak louder. All of those things together create huge misunderstandings that we don't always stop to challenge.

It's natural and important when looking at the subject of communication to begin with ourselves.

How I Saw Myself

I have always seen myself as a bright, caring person who loves to have fun. I am somewhat disorganized, forgetful, and often scattered. When I started learning about communication by looking at the model on time/communication, I noticed a lot more about myself, the most disturbing of which was my need to "please people."

People laugh today when I tell them, "I am a recovering people pleaser." However, it is no laughing matter to me. I spent thirty-plus years of my life trying to please everyone else (which didn't work, by the way)—to the extent that I truly did not know what I liked or wanted to do. I had given up so much of what was important to me. It was rather humbling to come to that place of understanding about myself and to be willing to take the first step toward true freedom by learning to speak what I was actually thinking instead of being silent or watering down my thoughts so no one would be offended. The journey to learning how to communicate effectively became extremely personal and important.

The lessons I teach now on how to say "no" were lessons I had to practice, as well as those about how to be open, honest, direct, and passionate without fear. Add learning to handle conflict and confrontations and building my self-confidence to my list of lessons, and you will have a pretty good understanding of why I am so passionate about resolving conflict, building trust-filled relationships, and communicating in an open and honest way.

I have not lost my sensitivity and concern for others, which is why sometimes I am edgy or unwilling to let others off the hook in terms of seeing the truth of their situations. I'm still scattered and disorganized, and on occasion too sensitive—no excuses, just being me! However, today, I view myself as more confident, more capable of speaking the truth in love, and better able to handle conflict and confrontation with grace.

How Others Saw Me

Until I started learning about the Time Communication Model, I would have sworn that others saw me exactly the way I saw myself. Wrong!

It is amazing what you become aware of when you intentionally reflect, watch, and listen. My family and friends saw both positive and negative qualities and behaviors in me early on that I did not see. My sister reminded me that I either kept myself buried in reading books or playing the piano from age four on. It got to the point that our parents put the piano in the bedroom we shared. I apparently wanted to play it all the time, and many of those times not appropriate in the opinion of the rest of my family. I remembered my sister used to lock me outside in the summer so that I would do other things besides reading or playing the piano. I spent countless hours playing cowgirl, riding my broom horse, and climbing trees—but she never saw that imaginative and playful side of me. Additionally, I have already recounted the differences of opinion in the situation where I saw rejection from my mom, while they saw favoritism.

In more recent years, I have become acutely aware that others see what I consider endearing qualities or behaviors as negative when done in excess. For example, I love people, and I love giving. However, recipients of that excessive love and giving see me as controlling. I have even been accused of trying to "buy someone," which was a very painful thing to hear. My need to see purpose before engaging in a task (an Imaginist trait) has also been seen as an attempt to control. I will speak more about the issue of control later on, but for now, I encourage you to ponder your own positive qualities and behaviors and how they may come across to others when used in excess.

Why So Much Misunderstanding?

From the Time Communication Model, I have learned that perceptions cause much of our misunderstanding. I have used data gathered with my five senses as well as my personal filters to form perceptions about myself and my life. But every person I encounter filters the same data through their own five senses and perceives something completely different.

How do we ever manage to connect on anything in life?

Misunderstandings occur every day in a myriad of ways. Communication includes more than just words. Often our actions, reactions, or lack of reactions speak louder than our words. That is why I often say actions speak louder than your words, particularly when they do not match.

It is easier for us to recognize our genetic perceptual differences of being focused or diffused. If you are an Analyst, you have probably found yourself wanting to say, "Focus!" or "Come back!" to Imaginists like me. I know I have wanted to say to tell Analysts, "Enough already on the details. I've got it!" But what the Windows have taught me is that our greatest misunderstandings occur because of our perceptual differences of continuous or discontinuous viewing of the event. It is so easy for me just to disconnect and move on when many of you want to continue trying to connect all the dots. I want to say, "Who cares?" but I do not because I have learned that you do care. When thinking about this, I can recall John Davies repeatedly saying, "We are just human beings being human."

I think one of the biggest lessons I have learned from the Windows is to eliminate judgment and walk in love by letting my friends, family, and co-workers be human, or in other words, who they were created to be. One of my favorite ways of describing this is to say, "Different is not bad; it is just different."

So join me on my quest to erase as much misunderstanding as possible and seek clarity in our interactions with one another. But you will need to start by understanding yourself before you can apply it to others. As you ponder your own results of the Time Communication Analysis, do not judge yourself or the results too quickly. Allow the results to prove their own validity by reflecting, asking others, and intentionally becoming aware of how you say and do things. Self-awareness is key to wholeness. I am constantly challenged, even thirty years later, to practice it daily and actually to see it as fun. I hope you will too.

What Is My Responsibility?

Being a great communicator requires a healthy "emotional intelligence." Emotional intelligence starts with self-awareness.

Attending that time management workshop those many years ago was the beginning of my journey to self-awareness—a journey that has continued right up to today.

I believe writing this book has been part of my journey as well. I have always stated that my purpose in life is "to turn people's lights on." Seeing the light go on when someone else receives a revelation is so exciting to me. Living a life "on purpose" is fun. There is no greater feeling than to be teaching, coaching, and watching, as the people you are living life with grow, change, and become everything they were created to be.

Do not get me wrong. Getting to that place where I clearly understand my purpose and have figured out how to fulfill it has taken time. For you, taking the Time Communication Analysis and reading this book may be part of your journey of self-awareness. It is a journey I hope you are already on and, if not, one that you are willing to start.

After learning to practice self-awareness, the second level of emotional intelligence is self-regulation. Learning about myself, my strengths and weaknesses, and how I impact others does not give me license to continue making mistakes without taking ownership. Self-regulation leads me to manage my weaknesses, fixing what I can, asking for help where I cannot, and not using them as an excuse.

As I mentioned earlier, the biggest weakness revealed to me from my Time Communication Analysis was my strong tendency to be a people pleaser. That tendency has driven me for over thirty years and is one that I constantly have to guard against. There was one point in my life when I realized that I did not have a single thought or opinion of my own. I sought other people's opinions before I formulated my own, and most of the time I then chose their opinions. I ignored my own feelings, likes, and dislikes in preference of everyone else's, thinking that it was the "right thing to do." Yet, I always felt like someone was upset with me or like I was doing something wrong.

My faith has always been an important part of my life. As I was praying one day, I felt God saying to me, "Why do you buy other people's maps (or viewpoints) about who you are or how you act? You are taking on opinions which were never intended for you." Imagine the freedom that came into my life when I learned that I am who I was created to be and that learning to express and be that person was the only way I would ever reach my potential and find peace in my life. Now I am able to control my people pleasing tendency nearly all the time, except when it is triggered by being tired and not taking care of myself.

I have also come to realize that I need to be willing to meet others where they are and not just demand that they accept me where I am. That is how I developed the principle of communication that says, "If I approach you, I should be willing to change my communication to provide what you need in communication, and I ask that if you approach me, you should be willing to change in order to provide what I need." Saying what I need requires openness and willingness. Self-regulation also requires me to walk richly in my strengths and use those strengths in every relationship and area of my life to fulfill the purpose given to me by God.

I believe it is my responsibility to walk every day using what the Windows have taught me. I call it "love with feet on it"—being non-judgmental and seeking to bring clarity into every conversation. Understanding differences in the way people think and act brought me to a place of understanding that: "Different is not bad. It is just different." So rather than judging them or myself for being different, I am able to look for opportunities to bridge the gap of those differences and to see the value in everyone. Again, there is freedom in letting go of judgment of myself and others.

So what is my responsibility? First, it is to identify my strengths. I have my list. Now, it is your turn.

Assignment #1: List your strengths. Don't just write the list, however. Reflect on it, and determine if you are using those strengths. How much are you using them? Too little, too much, or like Goldilocks, "just right?" It's important to capture this information to see where you might need to make some adjustments.

Assignment #2: Write a list of your weaknesses. Reflect on it. Are there some you can fix? Then do it. If not, how do those weaknesses play out in your life? What resources can you use to conquer your shortcomings in those areas? Too long have we tried to "hide" our flaws, when strength comes from owning them and allowing others to come beside us to support us in their strengths. At ILD, we frequently recommend books by Susan Scott, leadership coach and founder of the global training company, Fierce, Inc., to our clients. I heard her once say, "We are hard-wired for connection." We need each other in order to be the strongest person we were created to be.

Assignment #3: What have you learned so far about perceptions, differences in styles of communication, and the needs of individuals that can change how you interact with others? How can you work to be non-judgmental? How can you bring clarity to conversations?

Chapter 2
Communication Models Can Be Annoying

If I hear one more time, "It's just your personality!" I think I will throw up! Where did this obsession with understanding personalities come from? I think there is a basic curiosity in us as human beings to want to make sense of our interactions. Unfortunately, this drives us to focus on personality rather than digging deeper into ourselves and our relationships to understand the whole person, including communication, which is a better predictor of behaviors.

Many of you may remember from your Psychology 101 days that there are five basic approaches used: biological, psychodynamic, behavioral, cognitive, and humanistic. The biological approach is concerned with the activity of the nervous system, especially the brain action in regard to hormones and genetics. The psychodynamic approach emphasizes internal conflicts, which are mostly unconscious. The behavioral approach is concerned with the learning process, especially with each person's experience regarding rewards and punishments. The cognitive approach studies the mechanisms through which people receive, restore, retrieve, and otherwise process information. The humanistic approach emphasizes individual potential for growth and the role of unique perceptions in guiding behavior and mental processes.

How long have these approaches existed? The biological approach was founded by Charles Darwin in 1859 and was then modernized in the 1950s by the Wilder Penfield. The psychodynamic approach is credited to Sigmund Freud, and the behavioral approach was first discussed by Ivan Pavlov and B.F. Skinner. While Plato was the earliest to debate the cognitive approach, the modern day understanding of it was credited to Ulric Neisser in 1967. Finally, the humanistic approach was developed by well-known psychologists, Carl Rogers and Abraham Maslow.

By looking at this information and then reading again John Davies' discussion of the topic, it became apparent to me that he used all five approaches to develop his understanding of human behavior and to design the Time Communication Model. He also researched information from Richard Buckminster Fuller regarding time, which led him to using time as a point of reference. Then he added his theories about the changes that occur when an individual is under time pressure, which drives his model farther away from just being a "personality" instrument.

Overuse of Personality

Have you taken a stroll on Facebook lately and seen the number of tests you can take to tell you more about your personality? Their titles are things like: What Type of Flower Are You?; What Kind of Human Are You?; What Color is Your Aura?; What Career Should You Actually Have?; and What Type of Car Are You? Then there are the popular Myers-Briggs Type Indicator test, Minnesota Multiphasic Personality Inventory, DiSC Test Profiles, Team Dynamics Profile, Birkman Method, StrengthsFinder assessment, and KolbeA Index, just to name a few. There are other tests with results that describe you as an animal, a color, a temperament, or—as one of the newest tests I have seen does—an archetype.

I think this is why I was so drawn to Davies' work. Instead of focusing on my personality, it was a way of understanding how my brain processes information, and thus, it could predict with great reliability how I would react, communicate, and behave. Frankly, when people start pointing out my personality traits (usually in a negative way), I get offended. How about you?

It is important to point out that I believe all of the above inventories I referenced above can have a place of value in self-discovery. What I find the most disturbing, however, is how they are misused by organizations and individuals in attempts to categorize or box in an individual.

I have learned from the Windows that, while you can see certain personality characteristics in each Window, if you focus on that trait (which so often is a learned behavior), you may miss noticing the way a person actually processes information. This may lead you to use the wrong Window to communicate with them. That's part of the reason I say that you will see yourself in every Window. In the years I have used the material, fewer than ten people have had a score of 0 in any Window. You and I can both go to any Window at any given time. We just like to stay in our preferred Window. So personality can get in the way of understanding ourselves and other people fully if that's the only thing we focus on.

Word Definitions

For years, I have tried taking other communication or personality tests and have struggled to agree with the results. What the Windows have taught me is that this has to do with word definitions. When asked to choose between two words, I make my choice, but when I get the results, they seem so different from who I think I am. Later, I often discover that my definition of the word is different from the test's intended definition. What a revelation this realization was to me.

That is another big issue: when miscommunication or misunderstandings happen, they are often over word definitions. One of the first times I really saw this was when I was doing some work with a married couple on goal setting.

The husband, who was a big Imaginist, said, "In the near future, I would like for us to buy several acres of property to build on."

His Producer wife reacted almost in anger. "What do you mean? We are so far in debt that we can't buy any property!"

I stopped them and asked, "What does 'in the near future' mean to you?"

The husband responded with five or six years. The wife laughed as she said, "Thirty days!"

See how simply the argument was avoided and the misunderstanding cleared by seeking clarity and understanding the different time views of the Windows? If only we practiced asking for clarity instead of jumping to conclusions or resting on the assumption that we mean the same thing.

Here is another classic example of differences in word definition. A few years ago, I was working with a gentleman, and we were traveling out of town. As he was leaving his house, his Producer wife asked, "Do you mind if I check into getting the car painted while you are gone?"

He answered, "Sure." From his Analyst viewpoint, that meant getting some quotes.

When we returned, I dropped him off at his house around dusk. He later told me that when he walked in the door, his wife was standing there grinning.

"Did you see it?" she asked.

When he replied, "See what?" she announced, "I painted the car."

You heard it right. She painted the car. She called a few places, asked how to do it, rented a sprayer, and painted it outside under the trees. Never mind the pollen and tree particles—she got it done! They had very different word definitions for "check on getting the car painted."

There is a very popular spiritual or ministry gifts inventory which I have taken. In my mind, my natural gift is teaching. It's what I do and what I love doing. However, in the inventories I have taken, that gift comes up as my lowest. So I went on a journey of trying to understand how they define each gift. My lowest communication Window is Analyst, and when I studied each of the inventories, I found they used Analyst words to describe a teacher. Duh! No wonder I scored low as a teacher. I do not respond to Analyst words, and my definition of teaching did not match theirs.

We complicate word definitions further with the fact that we can change verbs into nouns. We turn communicate into communication, manage into management, perceive into perceptions, and educate into education.

This applies to more than just the English language. I have been working with a colleague to translate the Time Communication Analysis into German. If you thought English was complicated, try matching definitions from the English language to those of the German language. It certainly is taking more than one attempt—I think we are working on the second or third version of the analysis now and are beginning to test for validity. No wonder communicating takes work.

Fear of Being Exposed

Throughout my years of working with the Windows, I have been surprised by the number of people who balk at even answering the Time Communication Analysis, argue over its findings, and often admit, after much discussion, that they did not answer it honestly. Why does this happen? I have come to believe it is because of an unconscious fear of being exposed. It is not always easy to love ourselves through all of our faults, and we spend many years hiding them from ourselves, as well as from others. Taking a communication or personality questionnaire can be exposing. What if it nails me? What if I have to admit I am really like that? What if I am wrong about what I am like?

Remember when I said that learning the Windows was life-changing? Well, I discovered that it doesn't matter how hard you try to skew the answers or how well you think you have hidden your true self from others or yourself. You tell everyone everyday who you are by your communication and behavior.

If we all took the time to read the clues in front of us and apply the simple lessons we can learn from the Windows, communication would become less complicated. The biggest benefit is that when we truly understand each other and are willing to serve the other person's needs before we demand the fulfillment of our own needs, the tendency to be judgmental goes away. We understand that different is not bad—it is just different—and we can become less frustrated in our communication and instead celebrate each other. Let go of fear as you continue to learn more about yourself through the Windows while reading this book. Love yourself and others unconditionally—remember that communicating through the Windows is "love with feet on it."

Fear is not worth the effort we give it. I have learned from the Windows to stop giving room in my mind and emotions to fear and to start looking and listening through the lens of love. I can't tell you I am perfect at it (and I probably never will be), but it is a lot more fun to keep trying that than to walk around listening to fear. And as you know by now, fun is important to me.

Labels

We have complicated our world by trying to simplify it with labels. We want to label everything from habits, resulting in "workaholics," to behaviors like "ADD and "ADHD," which have now been designated as disorders. We classify things we don't understand and put people into categories by using labels such as "introvert" or "extrovert," "aggressive" or "assertive," Producer or Teamist.

No one likes being labeled or, as I often say it, "put in a box." This happens more frequently today than it did in the past, and much of the time it is wrapped around our personalities. This is why I found the Time Communication Model so refreshing. It is not about my personality but about the way I think and process information. It is less offensive—as long as it is not used to beat someone up with their faults or used by an individual as an excuse to avoid accountability.

In writing the Windows material, John Davies used labels to identify each Window, but he provided the following justifications, which I re-read recently. I thought you might enjoy seeing his thought process.

Producer: used to describe the person whose time preference is the present and who is driven by the intensity of their focused perception process, combined with the discontinuous perception process. Davies described Producers as "people capable of concentrating intensely on today's needs, or on a moment at hand, with a focus on distinct and separate individual tasks, plus an ability to handle them in a 'one-at-a-time' discontinuous manner." He went on to add, "By focusing their attention, energy, and skills on individual tasks and with discrete intensity, Producers will obviously produce better quantitative results."

Imaginist: used to describe the person whose time preference is the future. Their diffused perception and discontinuous perception enable them to visualize an extraordinary number of imaginative options and potentials. He described them as "having the ability to create mental variations and choices in terms of future outcomes as a direct result of a qualitative and expansive view of time." He went on to add, "Imaginists are accomplished visionaries of potential futures, capable of 'seeing' the whole design at the sacrifice of specifics."

Teamist: used to describe the person whose time preference is the past. By coupling their diffused perception with the continuous perception, they develop a preference for the qualitative aspects of situations, tasks, and activities, plus a respect for the traditional values of "times gone by." He described them as "having both the skill and ability of people sensitive to the human values, beliefs, and feelings in each living experience confronted in human existence as it evolves out of the past contributions of fellow beings."

He went on to add, "Teamists place a high value on creating time for people, feeling-tones, and changes of mind."

Analyst: used to describe the person whose time preference of a balance of the past, present, and future. Analysts have an acute focused perception process, which when joined with a continuous perception process, develops their ability to concentrate intensely on selective experiences, tasks, or situations with a focus on distinctive elements present in the experience. They then order the experience into a logical sequence of rationed-time priorities. Davies describes them as "able to create a continuous and balanced flow of applied effort, producing measured, quantitative accomplishment results from this analysis of experience." He went on to add, "They are accomplished in their ability to process experiences into linear programs of measuredprecision."

He was definitely a brilliant man of many words, wouldn't you agree?

Labels do not have to define who we are. They can be helpful in bringing clarity or in helping us to understand situations and interactions. I caution you to remember that very few people have a zero in any Window pane, so we can find ourselves in any of the four Windows at any given time within a day. We just develop preferences (our "like" defaults), which we automatically rest in whenever possible. This can help explain how sometimes you may have a full-blown conversation with someone and get an answer (you think) to a question you had. Then when that person has more time later, he processes the event through his default Window, and all of a sudden, he wants to rethink the issue or he questions what you had thought was already decided.

This happened to me recently. I engaged in a conversation on the phone while working more in my Teamist Window frame of mind, and we made a joint decision on how to proceed. After the conversation ended, my default Imaginist Window took over, and I texted a thought in the form of a question. It was a random thought with no particular agenda, and in a typical, curious Imaginist way, I fired off the question. Boy, did that set off a firestorm of confusion with the Analyst I had been talking to before, who couldn't understand where I was going with the thought. The waves of misunderstanding are slow to subside even now. (See how easy misunderstandings can happen because of differences in thought processes?) I hope that I learn from my own mistake of acting too quickly on a thought and that this story helps you avoid similar misunderstandings in the future.

Sorry for the rabbit trail (another Imaginist trait). Let's get back to labels.

Please use the labels of the Windows with caution. Can you see how I am referencing them as part of my thinking process, not as who I am? I think that can be healthy. My Windows preferences do not define who I am—they define how I think. Healthy emotional intelligence allows me to take that information and adjust it accordingly to reflect in my behaviors and attitudes. The labels of the Windows are designed to help bring clarity and to identify for you the filters that you or another individual is using, so that you can adjust your communication to fit his or her filters. For me, it's fun to see if I can get there. The benefits when I do are less frustration, less misunderstanding, greater clarity, better results, and an incredible peace of mind when relationships are stronger. I feel validated, and hopefully the person I am interacting with does too.

I want to show you how my team uses labels within our group. We never use them to be critical or condescending but to bring light to our current situations and to help each other understand where we are or what we see. It is not uncommon for someone on my team to say to me, "Come back, Miss Imaginist!" or "Are you going to your Producer Window?" I have even said to them on occasion, "I'm in my Teamist Window today." I have a really strong Teamist that works on our team, and I sometimes have to remind her not to let the Teamist get in the way. This signals her to step into her Analyst

Window and look at the situation with logic rather than the emotion of her Teamist Window.

It is so refreshing to see labels used without offense. I do again caution you, because not every person is always at the same level of understanding the Windows labels. I remember one time I called someone out whose Producer was running overtime and got my head chewed off. I failed to remember that this person was outside of our team and did not use the material as much as we do, so the label was offensive to them. I know a few Analysts, too, who hate to be called one. What is the saying from Shakespeare? "The lady doth protest too much, methinks"?

Assignment #1: Are there any traits (like speed of speaking or eye contact) that you exhibit which are different from your primary or secondary Window? How does that sometimes confuse others and cause communication issues?

Assignment #2: Over the next week, ask for clarification regarding word definition when communicating with someone you believe to be in a different Window than you are. Record your findings.

Assignment #3: Is there fear associated with being who you are? What have you been pretending not to know about yourself? And, as Dr. Phil would say, "How's that working for you?"

Assignment #4: Journal your personal thoughts about labels. How have you used them positively or negatively in the past, and what were the results you saw? How might you use labels differently now?

Chapter 3
Producers Are the Easiest to Understand

Producers are easy to understand, yet they are sometimes the most misunderstood Window of all. Seems like irony to me. They are the most straightforward communicators. They say what they mean and mean what they say, even though it sometimes appears as if they do not listen to their own words.

As a quick reminder, Producers combines a focused view with a discontinuous view which allows them to process everything that happens through the present time frame. This means they view their world as a Polaroid snapshot. As you read this chapter, keep in mind that it is written from the perspective of a "pure" Window. In other words, I will write as though none of the other Windows or their characteristics exist in a Producer. So you will not necessarily see all of these characteristics in yourself or another individual who has this window as a preference, because everyone is influenced by their interactions with the other Windows as well.

Before I learned this material, this was the one Window that would bring me to tears most often, especially when I was walking in every weakness of the Teamist. Producers tend to talk loudly, which sounded like hollering to me. They also talk quickly, and it always seemed like they were trying to pull something over on me. Lastly, they use a lot of action words, which came across as too demanding to me. How refreshing it was to learn that Producers spoke this way because they had a short period of time to say what was important before racing off to save the world or accomplish something big.

Let's look at how their thought processes work together to form their perceptions. They are focused on what is right in front of them, and they see each event as a single item without connecting dots between events. It can be said of them that "the squeaky wheel gets the oil." They see things from a time perspective of the present. There is only today, and everything on their list needs to happen now. This creates the urgency and speed with which they proceed through each day. They have a strong tendency to see each task as easy and something that should not take more than "five minutes," which puts them in a constant state of high expectations for themselves and others to get things done. Producers desire to be efficient, but their ability to carry through on this depends on the strength of their Analyst Window (see Chapter 6 on Analysts). They do not always connect the dots on their lack of efficiency, however, so do not waste your time trying to convince them of the truth. The higher the intensity of the Producer Window, the more zealous they can appear.

Producers are constantly "in motion." I traveled with one on a regular basis for over a year. He could not sit still for very long before his leg would start bouncing or he would begin humming. Usually, he would leave me in the dust as he sprinted ahead. He would work on his computer until the very last second before getting on the plane, which would sometimes make him the last passenger to board. I learned just to move at my own pace and not fret about where he was or if he was going to make it.

Now, I work with another Producer who is always in a hurry, especially at the end of a trip to get home, so he often sprints ahead of me. Several times we have laughed together, as I end up at the same bus stop as him despite his hurried pace. A couple times, I have waved from my bus as he was left standing at the stop because it was too full. He calls me the turtle, and I call him the hare, all in good fun.

You have to love those Producers. They can get things done, and I am so thankful for that. "Move out of their way and let them go," I say. John Davies used the label "Producer" to describe the natural gifting they have to make things happen. However, do not fall into the trap of believing that means they are the only ones who can produce results. Other Windows can produce results, just in different ways and not always as quickly.

One interesting revelation I have had about Producers has to do with the differences in their behaviors when they are walking in weakness or have lower self-esteem. I have come to understand that we all manifest negative behaviors in order to hide our own feelings of insecurity. In a Producer this comes across as self-centeredness. In other words, they exhibit strong tendencies to make everything about themselves, and they strive to be the center of attention. Whenever you are tempted to say about a person, "He is so self-centered!" be aware that you might be seeing an insecure Producer.

It's *Not* About Control

I think it is only fair to say up front that, while it may appear that Producers have a control issue, it is not about controlling people from their perspective. They do, however, prefer to control situations around them, and they work best alone. Other Windows view this as control of people, but usually people are the last thing on Producers' minds when a task is standing before them (unless someone is in their way). Rather, Producers believe they can get tasks done faster and better than anyone else, and they are not afraid of hard work. They feel great when they can view all of their accomplishments at the end of a day. They never intend to disrespect another person; they simply want to get the job done. I once heard someone describe a Producer as a parent who was constantly grabbing a child to keep him or her from being hit by a bus and then promptly running to catch another child. They sometimes are not conscious of anything but the task in front of them, and the urgency of the day dictates the speed they are working at.

The next time you see a Producer coming toward you in a whirlwind to work on the same task you are engaged in, step back and let them do what they need to do. Do not take anything personally, because they don't intend it that way. Smile, and see their joy as they "get 'er done"!

It can also help at times to stop them long enough to see what's on their list. If your boss, for example, is a Producer, they may need to be reminded of all the items they have placed on your list one at a time and which they promptly forgot but still expect to be done in "five" minutes. They will not be offended if you seek clarification on the tasks and ask for their input on the priority of those tasks. In fact, they actually respect those who stand up to them.

"Usefulness" Is the Key

Producers listen for usefulness. To them, usefulness occurs only in their current situation. They do not have time to listen to something that is for a later time than today. They are not being rude; it is just not useful information to them. So if you are going to talk to a Producer, limit your information to answer the questions "what, how, and when" for the current situation. They talk and listen fast, so you have only a short time before their attention has moved on to something else. Again, they do not intend to be rude. It's just difficult for them to slow their thoughts down long enough to listen.

They have a very short "short-term" memory, so do not be put off if they cannot recall something that happened last week or even yesterday. They disconnect quickly and are focused on the next item. Sometimes Producers bumper car their way through a day and do not even realize they are doing it. Anything can distract them and make them jump to another task—thus the reference to bumper cars. They may start a task, but if the phone rings, someone stops them, or even if they look up and see another task on their desk, they will bumper car from the task at hand to the next one without completing the first.

They naturally set priorities by stacking them. In my old banking terms, they live by LIFO (last in, first out). This usefulness filter explains why they leave things lying around. That spot is where they used it last, and they will probably need it again there. Why bother putting it away when they will need it again soon? Remember, usefulness is their filter in making every choice, whether that choice is what the quickest way to go is, what they should eat, or what they should wear. This is where they begin to add the word "practical" to the reasoning for their choices. In fact, some of their favorite words beside the obvious ones like "hurry," "do it," and "handle it" are "practical," "efficient," "necessary," and "simplify." They also prefer speaking in first-person terms, emphasizing the "I," "me," and "mine."

Their filter of usefulness also affects their personal and work space environments. Their desks may be cluttered with stacks—they know what is in each one—or leftover items which might still be useful, such as nuts and bolts, magazines, cloth for sewing, or old glasses. Other items you might see in their homes or offices are such things as: trophies, taxidermy, varied samples of handicraft or hobby work, "realistic" paintings or pictures, and sports items.

Passionate vs. Rude

Producers are by far the most passionate people I have met. They are driven by strong beliefs and values which create urgency for all they do and say. This passion adds to the volume with which they speak and causes others to think they are yelling or being rude, though this is not their intention. They are just sharing with gusto or passion, and the more their passion grows about what they are saying or doing, the more their volume naturally rises. They truly are unaware of how loud they have become in their excitement to share their news or findings with you.

The other aspect that causes us to see them as "rude" is their short sentence structure. The words "go," "get," "do," "hurry," and "now," accompanied with their volume equates to rudeness from my Teamist perspective. Plus, they have a propensity for saying, "You need to!" The Imaginist in me hates having anyone to tell me what I need to do or how to do it, increasing my conviction that the Producer is being rude.

I have learned through my study of the Windows to give Producers grace, not to take it personally, and to help them become self-aware. I think that, of all the Windows, I now enjoy working with Producers the most because they are so easy for me to understand.

Another point to consider in the issue of Producers being passionate versus rude is their tendency to run late. They are so passionate about their tasks that they lose track of time and think they can do one more five-minute task before leaving for their next meeting, and then they end up being late. Many translate this as rudeness, but again, there is no intent of that from the Producers. They just lost track of time. They also overcommit because they are not able to accurately assess how long something is going to take them to do. I have worked with several Producers on their to-do lists and found that on one day they had tasks totaling ten hours of work, which they expected to get done in seven. Imagine their surprise. Producers can be prime candidates for becoming workaholics, though in fact they love to engage in leisure time activities such as painting, gardening, ceramics, active and competitive sports, boating, woodworking, hunting, and sewing.

It's *Not* Personal

Producers tend to react quickly and without thought. Their discontinuous view of time drives this trait along with the intense pressure they feel from only having "today"! Thus, when an event happens to interrupt their task or focus, they react without thinking. In my years of working with the Windows and particularly with Producers, I often try and remind them to breathe or count to ten.

Recently, I learned of a technique intended to help change the thought process in the brain to lessen reaction. To try it, take your less dominant hand and squeeze it for ten seconds before reacting to something. Several of my Producer friends have tried it with some success. Another book I read suggested wiggling your toes for ten seconds before reacting.

The purpose of this discussion is to help those of you who are not Producers to understand that Producers do not intend their emotional blasts to be taken personally. Instead, their reactions are usually made without thought to the situation. We have had a lot of laughs in my office over a Producer blurting out in a class earlier this year, "That's just stupid!" to a high intensity Teamist. This Teamist might have walked away with hurt feelings, but she did not because of her understanding of Windows. She knew she was not stupid, although her statement had seemed stupid to the Producer. I know this Producer really well, and I know he would have been very upset at himself if he had hurt another individual. His comment was not personal.

Sometimes to other Windows it feels as if Producers are using words to pound their views into you. They interrupt you and might even walk away or hang up when they are finished talking—even if you are not. Again, it is not personal. They are just done and have moved on to the next task.

It probably would help to remind you that Producers do not read. They scan, looking for useful information. Do not send them a detailed report that is more than one page or an elaborate email with several subjects included. Producers tend to scan the first item and respond to the first item without reading the rest of the email. Later, they will swear they did not receive the additional information contained in the initial email.

Producers' lack of eye contact is also not personal. They cannot just sit and listen because to them it is a waste of time. Walk with them while you talk, or let them do something else while they are listening unless the information you are giving them is vitally important. Then call that fact to their attention, and give them a time frame for how long you need them to stop what they are doing and listen to what you are saying. Once you start talking, just give them the CliffsNotes version, not the whole story. You will really be testing them if you are long-winded or give them too much information. No matter how much you need that information, they really do not need it all. Remember: it is not about you. It is about what they need in order to hear what you are saying.

We need Producers because of their creative ability to figure out how to make something happen quickly. In teams, they bring great value by completing the tasks and bringing things to a conclusion. Just remember that once in a while you may need to remind them to let someone else handle something, to breathe, or to slow down. They will not be offended, as long as you do not take away their perceived control of the situation.

This leads me to one last thought: each Window has a natural gifting or strength. When that gifting or strength is used in excess, others tend to view use of that gift or strength as "control." This results in the perception that Producers are trying to control those around them, when they are only trying to "get 'er done."

Closing Thoughts on Producers

So, let's put some final thoughts together about our wonderful friends the Producers and about some of the general characteristics you may see in them.

Producers dress in practical clothes, and those clothes might be the same for their work and play. They don't mind bright colors but believe in only purchasing things for the best price. They can wear items beyond the point usefulness, failing to notice their holes or tears.

Finally, Producers tend to be motivated to high levels of achievement and excellent performance in their careers and occupations. They choose careers that keep them physically busy;

allow them to carry responsibilities for action or doing; provide opportunities for hands-on stimulation; and produce tangible results. In a generalized way, this can include careers or occupations like supervision, medicine (EMT, nursing, physical therapy), sports, civil service (police officer, firefighter), transportation (truck driver, train engineer, or airplane pilot), mechanical or technology (X-ray, welding, auto repair), outside jobs (farming, landscaping, working with animals, water activities), inventory or warehouse, construction careers (engineering, plumbing, electrical, maintenance, masonry), and hazardous or risk-filled occupations. The Producer's job can be anything as long as it includes movement and results.

Producers:
- Thrive on accomplishments
- Love sticky notes
- Are motivated by results
- Pay attention to bullet points and bolded information

Assignment #1: If you are a Producer, how can you become more aware of how your behaviors come across to others? Once you see it, how can you adjust?

Assignment #2: If you work or live with a Producer, where do you struggle the most in communicating with them? What changes could you make to reduce your frustration?

Chapter 4
Imaginists Are the Most Likely to Make Anything Fun

Imaginists love to have fun, and they have a keen ability to create a fun atmosphere in any task or event. If they cannot make it fun, they are not going to do it.

I have a very dear friend who is a strong Imaginist. In 1989, when Hurricane Hugo hit our area, she picked me up for an adventurous trip to the grocery store. Just getting there through all of the debris was one adventure, but the greatest adventure came at the grocery store where they were allowing a few people at a time to go in and shop even though the power was off. My friend turned the event into an absolute party. We had to stand for a long time in the checkout line as they were pricing and adding everything manually on a calculator. So she started opening snack foods and passing them out to everyone. Soon, she had us all laughing and singing as we waited. The cashier and manager thanked us for keeping everyone in good spirits as we ran out the door with our stuff. I could tell you many other stories of the combined Imaginist fun times we had during the years that we were neighbors.

So what gives an Imaginist the skill to create fun in everything? I think it is their ability to disconnect and see each event separately and their ability to leap into the diffused future of possibilities. To Imaginists life is an adventure, and they approach each day with anticipation as part of the journey. When they are walking in their strengths, this is awesome, exciting, and fun. But in their weaknesses, this quality can be depressing, negative and stressful. They often appear totally scattered to others, and they seem never to be paying attention or listening as they stare into space.

The comic strip "Family Circle" is such a clear depiction of the mind of an Imaginist. In one of them, the little boy is sent out by his mom to get his sister from the neighbor's house. But in typical Imaginist form, he wanders through the sandbox, pets the dog, throws a ball, takes a turn down the slide, hangs from the monkey bars, rides his bicycle down the driveway and back, and so on before he ever ventures next door to bring his sister home for dinner.

I am an Imaginist, and learning the material about this Window was so helpful to me. It gave me understanding as to why I did and still do things and helped me realize how others saw me (we have already discussed this, I know!). I often laughingly tell parents of children who are showing signs of becoming Imaginists to keep my number and call me when their children turn fifteen, because they will need some reassurance at that particular stage that everything will be okay.

It's *Not* About La-La Land

Imaginists are random thinkers. They do not think sequentially in terms of A, B, C, D. Instead, their thought process looks like this: A, B, G, L D, Y . . . . So it is natural for others to think they are wandering out in "La-La Land." This impression is further intensified by Imaginists' tendency to get lost in their thoughts and allow long periods of silence in the middle of conversations. I cannot tell you the number of times people have said things to me such as, "Where did you go? Are you still there? Come back to me, partner! Did I lose you?" All because I have wandered far into my mind about something they said.

The idea of La-La Land is also driven by the ability of an Imaginist to leap out into the world of possibilities and see everything as possible. It is kind of like going after Moby Dick with a fork in a row boat. Why not?

Depending on the influence of the other Windows in Imaginists' minds, they may need assistance in setting a roadmap to help them reach the possibilities; they just know it will work. I worked with a negative version of an Imaginist for a while. He was always sure something could not happen, or was not possible, or that the world was going to end. I lovingly called him "Eeyore." We had great work experiences together after he jumped into the positive side of possibilities and let go of his fear.

I have another dear Imaginist friend who is out to change the world. Any day now, the money will arrive to allow his plans to happen. I absolutely believe with him that this will happen, since his Analyst side is preparing the way with volumes of plans. Without people like him, Einstein, or Edison, who knows what this world would be like? I like traveling in those circles of possibilities, because they lead to ideas of something that might work. Thinking of new ideas is a whole lot more fun than sitting at a desk doing the same thing day in and day out or working on an assembly line. Not that there is anything wrong with assembly line work—It's not what me or any of my Imaginist buddies are cut out for. We need variety, dreams, opportunities, and change. Some of our favorite words are "What if . . .," "Let's try . . . ," and "Oh, my goodness, I just got this great idea . . ."

People are drawn to Imaginists because of their spontaneity. Unfortunately, this is also what drives other people crazy, because Imaginists cannot be pinned down to things. In weakness, they have difficulty making commitments because they want to leave the door cracked for other possibilities. John Davies affectionately called Imaginists "navel watchers." He said they could sit doing nothing and appear as if they are staring at their navels. Yet, in reality, they are wandering in a world of opportunities and dreams of where they could go and what they could be.

Learning to be a presenter was somewhat challenging for me as an Imaginist. I would jump from one thought to another and often go out of order, which totally lost some of the other Windows. I would lose track of time and find myself only halfway through my material when it was time to end. Learning this material about the different Windows helped me get other Imaginists to see how they were doing similar things and causing others to lose traction in their presentations, classes, speeches, etc.

I watched in one church as the Imaginist Pastor took off in a new direction during a sermon. One of the people in the congregation who was familiar with this material leaned over and whispered to me, "There goes the Imaginist." Being familiar with the Imaginist Window helped this pastor's congregation be more understanding when he would start preaching a series, teach only two weeks on the series, and then jump to something completely different. It also brought understanding to another organization when one of the church's programs was never implemented before the pastor moved on to something new. Imaginist leaders can be a challenge for their followers.

I used to absolutely paralyze my Analyst business partner whom I worked with for many years when I would throw out random ideas of what we should be doing as a company. He would get lost in trying to see the process of how my ideas would work, which of course I didn't know or care about. I finally realized that he was comfortable with the way we were doing things, and if I wanted to make any changes, I needed to do them slowly, methodically, and with a plan he could see. It's no wonder that since he has retired, I feel like a rubber ball bouncing around, trying to set a new direction for the organization.

"Purpose" Is Paramount

When an Imaginist does not see the purpose behind doing something, it is not going to happen. Without purpose, an Imaginist is lost. But watch how vibrant they become when the topic is centered on a purpose that has great meaning to them. I have an Imaginist friend who recently demonstrated this exact behavior. She has a passion for helping young women but had pulled back from those activities in order to focus her attention on getting her own nonprofit organization structured with the help of her board. During this time, she often talked about not feeling motivated and would describe herself as feeling disconnected. But when she was invited to help mentor young women through another organization, the tone of her conversation changed. She is now excited and filled with stories of how rewarding life is, because she found purpose again in what she is doing. I am so excited to see it.

The "why" question is so important to Imaginists, but this priority often alienates others. Imaginists are naturally curious, and when that curiosity is used in excess, others see it as trying to control or digging too much. I talked to a Curiosity Coach (a specialty coach who focuses on helping executives to become "curious" again) a few years ago who believes we have lost our natural curiosity. He works with executives to help them re-engage curiosity in their employees as a way of moving their organizations forward. To accomplish this, all they need to do is hire one strong Imaginist and let him go. If Imaginists' curiosity is stifled, they will retreat into their own thoughts or quit.

Imaginists can spot patterns quickly, assess when changes will bring a greater purpose to what is being done or when something serves no purpose. I am convinced that a lot of their procrastination occurs when the purpose is not clear or when they do not feel the freedom to question the apparent lack of purpose. A part of me also thinks a lack of purpose is what causes Imaginists to stop reading one book and start another. What is the purpose of finishing it when they can already see where it is leading? I cannot begin to tell you the number of books I have started and never finished because I had already found their purpose or never saw a purpose in them to begin with.

Imaginists spend a lot of time wandering through endless what ifs and why nots to determine purpose. Since purpose is their primary filter for listening, do not leave it out in your conversations with them. Allow periods of silence during your conversations as they process through your words. Do not be put off if they smile or laugh during serious times as they literally convert your words to pictures in their mind, all the while looking off into the distance. To some, this behavior seems rude and implies the Imaginists are not listening, but in fact the opposite is true. They are fully engaged and have no intent to be rude.

Disconnected vs. Connected

Like the Producer, Imaginists have difficulty connecting the dots because of the discontinuous process their brains use. They move from the most recent event to a diffused view of the future, so please cut them some slack when they seem to forget something important. I often look to the future and see something important like a birthday coming. Then I promptly move through life and forget to acknowledge the birthday when it finally arrives, although several weeks earlier I was looking forward to celebrating it. I buy cards sometimes a month in advance, and then I lose them in my piles of stuff and find them a month after I should have sent them.

Probably one of the most annoying traits of an Imaginist is how they trail off in the middle of a conversation. I am told that I frequently stop talking mid-sentence and leave the other person hanging. I believe it is my discontinuous way of thinking that causes me to disconnect and leap into another thought somewhere else. This is not meant to be an excuse or justification—it is just information to help others understand. I do not like doing it, nor do I believe other Imaginists do either. So if any of you come up with a way to stop it, please let me know (and saying, "Focus!" doesn't work).

Short-term memory is also impacted by this discontinuous process. Imaginists do not remember what they said a week ago, yesterday, or sometimes five minutes ago. The discontinuous view coupled with the diffused lens adds to the spatial thought process used by an Imaginist. This causes them not to communicate in a linear manner of A, B, C, D, but rather in the nonlinear sequence of A, B, C, Q, E, etc. Their thoughts then come across to others as rambling and having no substance.

I had an interesting conversation with a high Imaginist recently about her difficulty with thinking outside the box. This was no surprise to me, because as an Imaginist, she doesn't always see boxes. In fact, Imaginists detest boxes because they represent boundaries. Imaginists are demotivated by rules, regulations, limitations, and policies. One of the best Imaginist books I have ever read is one entitled Orbiting the Giant Hairball: A Corporate Fool's Guide to Surviving with Grace by Gordon MacKenzie. It is a great tool for Imaginists to use in learning how to stay engaged in corporate environments without becoming sucked into the vortex of policies, procedures, and rules most large corporations run by, thus losing motivation. Check it out—but realize that if you are not an Imaginist, it will probably be difficult for you to read.

Imaginists love to be challenged and will engage immediately in a project that has an element of challenge, freedom, and fun. Once they can see through the project in their mind to the end result, their motivation to complete it is deflated. Sometimes, many started projects sit unfinished because they is no longer fun or because they have disconnected and started something new. Do you have any unfinished projects at home or in your office? You just might be an Imaginist.

What keeps Imaginists engaged all the way to the finish line are consequences. Sometimes I have to create my own consequences to motivate myself to finish something, or else I need a "nagging" Producer at my ear—how I lovingly refer to one of my favorite Producers.

Naturally, Imaginists are not the best spellers, at least not until they learn to tap into the visual side of themselves. They do not phonetically learn to spell. The best teaching technique is to have them write the word three times, then close their eyes and visualize the word in their mind as it is written on the paper. Then they will be able to spell it.

Imaginists can also be very strong in mathematics, but they are weak on their ability to show their work. They can literally do the problems in their head and get the correct answers, but if someone demands that they write out each step of the problem, they can get the wrong answer because they miss a step. I cannot tell you the number of parents who have talked to me about their children being criticized by a teacher, accused of cheating on a test, or failed in a class because of these characteristics.

How wonderful it would be if our education system recognized the Windows and allowed students to learn using their natural abilities, rather than forcing them into a box of accepted processes. I believe in learning, growing, and educating through creativeness. I do not believe in doing or learning by rote; repetition bores me.

The Need for a Challenge

I often remind bosses that if they have a strong Imaginist employee, it will be challenging to keep them motivated. This is not a negative quality at all; it is just difficult to understand if you are not an Imaginist. They can easily get bored with routine activities, and they enjoy being challenged constantly. It is not uncommon for Imaginists to change jobs often, with boredom being the most common reason. Unless a position remains challenging and changing, they will get bored and quit.

On the other hand, whatever is new, exciting, and different says "challenging" to an Imaginist. They can spend hours on a task and not even notice the time passing when they see an opportunity to develop something new, change something for the better, or explore the possibilities. Get a couple of Imaginists in the same room and watch the time fly by as they explore a myriad of topics together, taking numerous rabbit trails and laughing all the way.

Some Windows feel threatened when challenged. That is not the case with Imaginists. They enjoy being challenged. Just do not forget their propensity for giving a negative response the first time you throw out an idea to them. Over time, they will arrive at the positive. That is why we recommend using the "go fishing" technique with an Imaginist. If you want to get an Imaginist to discuss an idea you have, throw out the idea without discussing it and leave them alone for a while. If you try and discuss the idea immediately, all you will hear is why it will not work. However, if you allow them time to think about it, they will work through the negatives, begin to see the positives, and be ready to discuss the possibilities.

Pure Imaginists love conflict because they see it as an opportunity to dialogue, collaborate, or cooperate. It is the influence of other Windows that impact their ability to deal with conflict. For example if an Imaginist works with a strong Producer who is not willing to listen to any other person's opinion, the Imaginist will shut down or disengage completely. If an Analyst overloads the discussion with details, facts, numbers, etc, again an Imaginist will disengage. Finally, if a Teamist becomes overemotional, taking everything personally, an Imaginist will retreat into his or her thoughts and stop communicating.

Imaginists' love of a challenge can also lead them to be competitive. They love to win, and they see games and contests as a fun challenge. When I worked in financial institutions and they ran contests for new business, I either won or came in second every time. I was driven to stay on top. As I have aged, however, winning has become less important and just playing to have fun has taken priority.

I have also learned that when an Imaginist is walking in weakness and has a lower self-esteem, they will show attitudes or behaviors, which will cause you to want to call them "Arrogant." They are not really arrogant. Rather, they are deflecting their insecurities by overcompensating with their knowledge about everything. This comes across to others as being a "know it all" or extremely arrogant.

Closing Thoughts on Imaginists

Let's look at some general characteristics that we may see in Imaginist and some final thoughts about them.

They can be eclectic in their dress—fun, different, out of the box, and full of colors, but never concerned about mixing stripes, plaids, or polka dots. They also can get distracted while dressing and end up with two different socks, two different shoes, one earring, or even two different colors of eye shadow. Watching one of my young nieces growing up as an Imaginist, I loved how she wore her red cowboy boots with every outfit. Her hair would be pulled up on the side of her head in a ponytail, and she would wear polka dot tops with striped pants long before it was fashionable. She made everything she could hold in her hands into a microphone as she sang her way through the day.

Imaginists can excel in careers such as professional writing, research, art, advertising, college professor, musical writing and composing, and creative management in positions such as CEO or chairman. They thrive in design careers such as movie set and script design, interior design, hair design, landscape design, fashion design, design engineering, training and human resource development, and organizational development. Other popular fields include military or police intelligence, travel professions, space exploration, systems analysts, biology, medical research, and forestry work.

Imaginists have difficulty in listening to long presentations or people reading to them. They need pictures, color, and movement to keep them engaged in the conversation.

Imaginists:
* Appear messy and unorganized
* Lose things
* Save everything that might be useful in the future
* Constantly look for new ways to do things

Assignment #1: If you are an Imaginist, what weaknesses do you tend to walk in? Journal about these, and decide which ones you can fix and which ones you need to be aware of that may cause issues in working with others.

Assignment #2: If you live or work with an Imaginist, how can you adjust your communication to them to bring greater clarity? Consider using the "going fishing" technique. Journal your new understanding of them.

Chapter 5
Teamists Are the Most Willing to Work on Communication

Teamists are all about people and relationships, so communication is a high priority to them. This makes them very open to learning more about communication and to trying to understand more about others and themselves. The stronger the Teamist Window is in them, the more difficulty they have identifying another person's Window because they see Teamists in everyone.

I have very high scores in this Window, even though it is my secondary Window, but this was also where I walked in the most weakness. Learning about my Teamist weaknesses has had a profound impact on my life, though these were some of the hardest areas for me to conquer and change.

Let's look into Teamists' actual processing. They have a diffused view of their world, which is joined with their continuous view of each event. They need to connect what is happening in the present or the future with some past event. This makes them appear to walk through life backward, pulling the past with them into their present and future.

For Teamists, this process always involves people. Relationships are of top importance to them, which is why John chose the name "Teamist" to describe them. Their strength is their natural ability to form relationships and assess how a group is feeling. I often encourage leaders who are not strong in this Window to find a Teamist in their organization and let them know what is really going on within the organization. The Teamist can usually pinpoint pretty accurately how employees and customers or clients are feeling about the organization.

Their perception process gives them their long-term (elephant type) memory, although they will swear they do not have an elephant memory. I just remind them that their memory is selective. It is always connected to something of importance to them personally. They generally respond, "That's true!" They have strong ties to memorable and historically significant events. (For example, Teamists can tell you where they were when the Twin Towers were destroyed on 9/11.)

I believe Teamists helped to write most of the materials available on communication. How much have you been taught about the importance of your tone of voice, your body language, and eye contact? Those are all key components for communicating with a Teamist. Unfortunately, they are also the very things that can cause confusion with the other Windows when they are relied upon as practices of good communication.

Teamists place high value on the use of time to all living experiences, personal relationships, communal activities, and "feeling-level" communications. They are personable, romantic, sentimental, and totally people-centered. They require extra time for talking to others, bonding, helping others, and learning as much as they can about those around them.

It's *Not* About You Personally

No matter how many times you say to a Teamist, "It's not personal," it is very hard for them not to listen to those words because Teamists filter everything personally. Their continuous view causes Teamists to link all events together and apply the results or consequences of those events to themselves, even if they were not involved.

As a Teamist, I can get more upset over the poor way I think another person is being treated than I might for myself. It may seem crazy to you, but my Teamist is so strong that I take on other people's emotions all the time just by walking past them, talking to them, or over-identifying with them if someone else is talking about them. Another Teamist will understand when I say, "We can feel the vibes when we walk into a room."

I probably drove my son insane in his teenage years, because I was always "reading" his body language, often incorrectly, and thinking he was upset about something when he wasn't. The conversation would escalate to him almost yelling at me, "There's nothing wrong—leave me alone!" To which I would promptly reply, "Then notify your face!" How he survived me, I do not know.

Teamists look at the recipient list of a group email to see what order names are listed in, who is copied, and how the overall tone of the correspondence is. Offense comes easily. They prefer face-to-face communication so they can assess your facial and body expressions. They are also touchy, meaning they like to pat you on the arm, hold your hand, or sit close to you. They are not trying to invade your personal space—it's just natural to them.

I have learned to not take things so personally most of the time; however, I have also discovered that when I am tired, this weakness raises its ugly head, and I take everything you do or say personally. Hurt feelings were common for me in the past, which is part of why the Windows have become so important to me. I now have better control over myself and do not allow unnecessary hurt or resentment build up, which is so freeing. I have even learned to dialogue openly in order to seek clarity when something is said and I realize I am taking it personally.

"Personal Value" Brings Clarity

Teamists' listening filters are based on personal value. This means that when listening or reading, they process the words, tone of voice, and body language to see if the subject relates to them personally or has personal value to them. In strength, this is a tremendous quality because it gives them a sixth sense of what is going on and a great gift for discernment. In some respects, they listen through their heart and gut, not just through their brain. This also gives them the ability to recognize quickly how others are feeling or how they are perceiving communication. I have always found it important to identify the strong Teamists working with me and use them as a thermometer to determine how the group or organization is feeling. Helping them stay positive can help the whole organization stay positive, since they are powerful influencers.

In weakness, Teamists' strong attention to another person's body language and tone of voice leads to frequent misunderstandings and hurt feelings. They have a tendency to think Producers are yelling at them all the time, Analysts are mad at them, and Imaginists don't respect them—all because they have this natural tendency to take things personally.

It was a very strong Teamist who taught me the importance of asking for clarity by saying something like, "I know what that means to me. What does it mean to you?" I have used this tool now for many years and have found it to be very useful in bringing to light differences in perceptions and definitions.

It is important to be aware that Teamists can be "word sensitive," and their elephant memories come into play in regard to this sensitivity. They think in terms of "we," "us," and "our," and they are often put off by the overuse of "I," "me," and "my." I find this extremely interesting because our personal value filter also causes us to often think everything is about us. I have to be reminded and to remind other Teamists: "The world is not all about you!" When someone says it to me, I want to gasp, but I quickly realize that I have subconsciously been taking everything personally or making it about me. This stern reminder helps bring me to greater clarity and peace.

Just this past week, my Teamist Window almost got me into trouble by reading between the lines and being sensitive to words. I walked away from a conversation after a meeting, thinking that I was no longer wanted as a board member of a nonprofit that I have been working with and serving for three years. I got into the car and, as I was driving, replayed all that was said and everything I heard between the lines. The end of that replay convinced me that I should resign because I was no longer wanted. My feelings were hurt.

But because I have grown so much personally from learning about the Windows, I knew better than just to react and leave it there, so I called one of the main people from the conversation and asked for clarity. He laughed and helped me not to read into anything and to see that my interpretation was completely incorrect. I was still wanted, needed, and very much appreciated as a member of the board. He was just trying to be sensitive to my schedule and to avoid overloading my schedule with the extra responsibilities of serving as an officer on the board.

Reading Between the Lines and Body Language

I am constantly amazed at how keenly Teamists can hear what is not being said. In strength, they are right, and in weakness, they are hearing or seeing things that are not there. For me, it is a constant challenge to remain centered and to read others' communication accurately. Being willing to ask open-ended questions and to seek clarity helps.

At ILD we often coach in pairs so that we can utilize the strength of our Teamist Windows. This helps us see and hear all that we need to see and hear in order to be most effective in helping our clients grow. If I am leading, the other coach invokes their Teamist Window to observe and hear what I might be missing. It is great to have that ability—as Teamists, we can do it alone, but we prefer to have company in everything we do.

There is another aspect of reading between the lines that I think warrants a discussion from the Teamist viewpoint. Teamists read between the lines, and therefore, they often expect you to do the same. This is evidenced by their communication styles, which are not direct but rather peppered with implied conditions. Instead of saying, "I need you to . . . " they say, "It would be nice if such-and-such happened." They feel that direct communication can be hurtful, so they try and soft pedal their way through their needs and/ or feelings. For many years, I would go home and complain that co-workers were not doing what I asked. Then the Windows taught me that I was not asking them to do anything. I was implying what I needed to be done, and they were not understanding my meaning. So Teamists, if things are not happening the way you would like them to, check your communication. You may not be making your requests in a direct enough way for others to get it.

Another way Teamists read between the lines is by interpreting body language—a practice that can yield mixed results.

Studying and watching body language has been a communication tool for years, but learning about the Windows has given me a new perspective on it. A recent article I read about body language suggested that if a person overly tilts their head and smiles, they are flirting with you. I do this frequently, but when I do, it is my inner Imaginist picturing what you are saying, which brings a smile or silent laugh to me. I wonder how many times someone has thought I was flirting when it was the furthest thing from my mind. This article also talked about looking into someone else's eyes. If they dart their eyes from side to side, they are nervous or distracted. But I have learned from the Windows that darting eye movements can indicate an Analyst processing what you are saying. Looking down means someone is upset or hiding something, according to the article, but the Windows tell me that behavior is often a Teamist connecting with their feelings or memories about what you are saying.

One of my favorite assumptions the article made about body language was that nervous gestures like pushing up your glasses on your nose can indicate disagreement. I thought it just meant my glasses needed to be adjusted. Then it said that tapping your toes means boredom, or that slow shuffling of your feet might mean you are uncomfortable. But I thought this was just a Producer who can't sit still. And finally, touching or pushing your hair back can mean you disagree with what's being said. Not sure this is true for me—how about you?

I suggest that you not take all body language research at face value but that you investigate it through the Windows, especially you, my Teamist friends.

It's *Not* About People Pleasing

Too many times I have said, "I'm a recovering people pleaser," without realizing the impact of that statement. The people pleaser is a part of me that I will never be able to completely get rid of. All I can do is minimize its impact on my behaviors, emotions, and perceptions. I have learned recently that the people pleaser is one of ten mental Saboteurs exist in everyone, according to Shirzad Chamine in his book Positive Intelligence. I now understand that the stronger the Teamist in an individual is who is walking in weakness, the stronger the people pleaser Saboteur will be.

With that in mind, I hope other Teamists reading this will be able to accept the impact of the people pleaser and take full advantage of the choices they can make every day in minimizing its impact. I have also realized that when I step into fear, I allow the people pleaser to take control because my fear usually involves not wanting to hurt someone's feelings or cause dissension. I never intend to lie, but rather to say nothing or to agree aloud, even though in my heart I do not. In the moment, I have been lulled into believing that is the best thing to do, not realizing that later, when my actions or words with others do not agree with what I previously did or said, it causes the very dissension I had been trying to avoid. What a revelation that was to me.

If you are not a Teamist, help those of us who are Teamists by giving us a safe environment to speak what is on our mind without fear of relationships being damaged. This becomes especially important when you understand that because of our continuous perception process, Teamists cannot separate disharmony in one part of their lives from disharmony in another part. That means if they are upset with something or someone at home they will carry that disharmony with them into their work and exhibit hurt, taking things personally and misunderstanding others' communication to them. They need help in separating their feelings and situations. Encourage us to learn to confront, and use open-ended questions to help us verbalize what we are really thinking.

Closing Thoughts on Teamists

Let's look at some characteristics that are common in Teamists as a final review of this Window.

Teamists hold onto things, especially in their closets. They may have items they wore twenty-plus years ago but cannot bear to part with, like favorite ties, football jerseys, or sweaters. They tend to wear warm but cheerful colors. They love hand-me-down pieces of jewelry.

They buy journals, notepads, and calendars by the feel of the item. In spite of technology, they often prefer paper calendars with quotations, pictures of living symbols (such as cats, dogs, mountains), or cute designs.

When setting priorities, they make choices based on whether or not they like or dislike the task. If I like it, I do it. If I don't like it, I don't do it.

Occupations that are typically viewed by a Teamist as "meaningful careers" include health or medical care; civil or governmental work; sales; artistry or theatre; banking or insurance; real estate; teaching; community affairs; personnel; sociology, anthropology, or psychology; religious and missionary fields; occupational therapists; and advertising or public relations.

Teamists:
- Can be ultrasensitive and take things personally
- Love to help others
- Can be slow to accept change
- Have keen discernment in understanding their environments

Assignment #1: If you are a Teamist, what have you learned about your tendencies that impacts your life the most? Journal about how you might adjust your communication and or listening style with others.

Assignment #2: If you live or work with a Teamist, journal your newfound understandings of them and how that can make a difference in your communication and relationship.

Chapter 6
Analysts Are the Most Likely to Be Thorough

Once you begin observing the Windows, Analysts will be the easiest for you to identify and to recognize what their needs are. They process information like a computer, and the stronger they are in this Window the more you will see their eyes dart from side to side while they are listening, almost like a flutter. They are thorough in everything they do, and communicating is no exception. This is the Window I tend to reject and is therefore the one I need around me the most. I would love to be able to process information the way Analysts do all the time, but if I do it for too long, I get a headache. I am just not wired that way. I am so glad I have learned that it is okay and that I can value them for their capabilities without having to become one.

A very focused view combined with the continuous view places the Analysts in the very unique position of needing all three time frames in order to form proper perceptions. They carefully look at the present to understand fully what it is. Then they go back into the past and chronologically compare every event they have experienced to see what led to the current or present event. Then, and only then, will they venture to look at the future. Because of their careful comparison, it is a calculated future, and they can now determine what the next logical step should be. That is probably what I appreciate about them the most—their thoroughness in assessing any given situation. The higher the intensity of this Window, the more thorough they become, and pressing them into faster action will not happen.

Some of my most important lessons about the Windows come from the Analysts, because they have been the most difficult for me to understand.

I loved my father-in-law dearly, and he was the most pronounced Analyst I have known. He loved order, and to be sure, it was well-maintained in his home. He tiled his garage floor and had cabinets built all along the walls of the garage. He drove the car each evening onto the tile, and then when he left the next morning, he expected that the tile would be wiped clean for his return that afternoon. We ate family meals in the garage once grandchildren arrived, so as to be sure the dining room remained spotless.

I also learned very quickly from being married to an Analyst that that you do not want to go along when they are shopping for Christmas trees or cars because of their extreme perfectionism. My brain struggles to process sequentially as they do, and I just want to skip ahead. Yet if I wait and listen to what they have to say, they have a complete set of reasons to present. One word of caution for them: at times they miss opportunities while working through their processes. I often see that when a very short time frame is available to make a decision, someone else may jump on the opportunity first, causing the Analyst's decision-making process to become null and void.

This thought process of the Analyst often leads them to be in their heads a lot instead of investing time in people. I have coached countless children of Analyst parents or employees of Analyst bosses. They all have so much to offer, but they were never given the time of day relationally speaking or were discounted because they didn't measure up to an unspoken perfection standard.

That's why I have used the book *A Peacock in the Land of Penguins* by B.J. Gallagher Hateley and Warren H. Schmidt and the training video based on the same material to help Analysts see how others sometimes perceive them. These training tools describe how Analysts have a tendency to be extremely demanding of others, requiring perfection sometimes beyond their capability. Too often these demands are unspoken and unknown to the others, which causes more confusion and hurt in communication. Analysts are the hardest on themselves, so they do not always see how hard they are on others as well.

Our world is driven by the values, beliefs, and standards of the Analysts, who have little grace to offer those who are, in the eyes of an Analyst, needy or scattered. One Analyst recently told me that, when speaking on a stage, I should only wear black to slim me down. Then recently, another Analyst also made a comment about the bright colors I wear. I love color, but I became so self-conscious that I started trying to wear only neutrals when I was going to be around this particular person. What a difference learning about my tendency to be a people pleaser made. It allowed me to recognize what was going on, and we actually discussed the issue, laughing together as we realized she actually loved the colors I wore when I thought she did not.

It's Not About CYA (Covering Your Assets)

"Document, document, document!" are favorite words of Analysts. This strong need for documentation led me to believe it was for the purpose of justifying their actions so that they would never be wrong. I understand now that they need to see it to believe it, and they think everyone else needs the same thing. While I cannot completely discount that some Analysts are using this practice in a negative way, documenting events is what they do. They do not need to prove they are right—they know they are.

ILD accumulated twelve years of tax records because no one could give my Analyst business partner a final answer on how long you need to keep them. I was so grateful when another associate introduced us to NeatDesk, a desktop scanner and form of organization software that allowed us to electronically keep those records and get rid of the paper records before they overtook my attic. I know that, as an Imaginist, I already keep too much, but that was overboard. Analysts are prone to hold on to everything. This partner retired three years ago, but recently, I was looking for something and called him. It was no surprise he still had a copy in his files. I love Analysts!

Their overwhelming amount of processing requires Analysts to document each step so that it can be reviewed for correctness and be available to follow in a similar future situation. I am convinced they can create processes out of anything.

Not convinced? Watch one pack the car for vacation.

A close friend told me about her Analyst husband packing the car for a trip, and just as the task was completed, a family member brought an extra item to go in the car. This required the entire trunk to be emptied so the item could go in the "right" place, thus delaying the start of their trip and throwing the Analyst's schedule completely out the window. If you live with an Analyst, you know that getting off schedule is never a fun experience.

The most fun example of documentation I can share is the story of how a caterer friend, who is a huge Analyst, once had to be away for an event. Ahead of time, he set a table just as he would for the event, added place cards with labels for what was to go in each place, and then took pictures to give to his staff who would be running the event in his absence. On a different occasion, I was teasing him about how he would use his thumb to measure the exact placement of the silverware on a table, and he showed me the pictures. Now that is documentation!

Order and Correctness Lead to Logic

It would be easy to say the last story should have gone under this topic and there is some logic to that as well. Do not fret, however—I have lots of examples. The listening filters of order and correctness are difficult to separate in Analyst minds. They listen for and look for order, and if any process is out of order, it is not correct. In the same way, if the results of a process are incorrect, it is because the process was done out of order.

The time required to process for order and correctness is what drives Analysts' need for a measured and metered tempo of conversation. Go too fast, and they cannot keep up with the process flow; go too slow, and they become agitated.

Their need for logic follows their need for order and correctness, and if they cannot see logic in an action, they will not do it. They are the most logical individuals I know, and it is easy for them to tell when any of the three—order, correctness, or logic—is missing in your conversation. Analysts will glaze over as they attempt in their heads to establish the order, correctness, and logic you apparently missed. This means they are not listening as you continue merrily on your way in conversation.

This listening filter also applies to their visual sides. I have learned before making a presentation to go to the back of the room and look at the front to be sure nothing has been placed incorrectly or out of order. If anything is out of place, the Analysts in the room will fixate on that and not on the presentation. I remember one time when my power point projection was slightly tilted. In the middle of the presentation, an Analyst got up to correct it for me. I really need them in my life!

The higher the intensity of this Window, the more unaware they seem of their need to adjust or correct anything out of order. They do not intend to hurt your feelings or call negative attention to you (in other words, it is not personal)—they just have to fix it. My Analyst husband notices every imperfection on or around me, all of which are unnoticeable to me. Though I often find this annoying, I have learned after twenty years that it is an automatic response, not an intended offense. Now, I choose to look at those times as a signal of his love for me, not a criticism of me.

In regard to Analysts' decision-making process, I like to say, "Analysts enter their cave to process the 'order and correctness' of what they are thinking. Until that process is completed and the next logical step is clear, very little communication goes on." Learning to give them this time to process can save the rest of us a lot of frustration. If they are in their "cave" too long, though, it does help to open the cave door and ask if there is anything you can take off their plates. This encourages them to process out loud, which often brings clarity more quickly for them.

Analysts can have two extremes in communicating. Sometimes, they hold cards close to their chest and do not communicate enough. Their other extreme is to communicate too much information, almost to the point of needing to tell you how the watch was made before they can tell you what time it is.

Over the years, I have tried to discern the differences between these two opposite styles. I have learned that when they do not communicate enough, it is because they believe others think in the same way they do and, therefore, should logically be able to figure out the needed information. I asked an Analyst once if what he was not telling me was a secret, and he told me, no, it just was not perfect yet, so he did not want to say anything.

In regard to the other extreme, I worked with an Analyst once who was compelled to tell you everything. In his case, nothing could convince him that you did not need to know all of it. He strongly believed that you could not understand a summary if you did not have all of the background information. Unfortunately, he eventually lost his job because his Producer boss could not handle the overload of information.

Since the thought process of an Analyst is so thorough, they have a built-in need to justify every one of their thoughts, actions, and decisions if they feel questioned in any way. It is another one of their unconscious reactions, which frustrates them if you bring it to their attention. They truly cannot see it.

I am so thankful for Analysts and their need to fix whatever is out of order around them. However, when this habit is used in excess, other Windows have a difficult time not viewing it as micro-managing every detail. I am convinced that Analysts' tendency to order and correct everything they see around them is an unconscious response, so we need to find a way to help them see the extremes in what they are doing without attacking them. Attacking only pushes them further into their non-communicative cave. Any Analyst who has experienced this kind of attack will understand how hard this is. I truly wish I could understand how it feels inside their cave.

Following a Process Is the Only Way

The influence of all three time frames drives an Analyst always to think in terms of a process. They cannot be spatial in thought but rely completely on linear, sequential thinking. I am so impressed with their creative ability to create a process out of anything almost immediately. While I say "immediately," I do not mean that the end result is always immediate, but the beginning of the process is. If the steps are unclear, they may get bogged down as they search for logic in what the next step should be. If they miss a step or find one out of order, it will result in an instant reboot to start over again since the process is flawed.

Another thing that causes an Analyst to reboot in conversation is an interruption. If you stop them mid-conversation to ask a question, they will answer the question and then go back to the beginning and start again. I thought this was meant to aggravate me, but I have finally learned that when their process is interrupted, they reboot and begin again. So, take it from many years of experience, and hold your questions to the end.

Once the process is determined, following it to the nth degree becomes completely necessary for them and for everyone around them if they want to please the Analyst.

One of the earliest stories I heard which reinforced this was about a non-Analyst father who argued constantly with his Analyst son at the dinner table. The father related one particular incident to me where the dinner consisted of meat, potatoes, and a vegetable. The food was positioned on the plate like a clock (meat at six o'clock, vegetable at ten o'clock, and potato at two o'clock). The father kept insisting the child eat some of his potatoes, but to no avail as the child ate all of his meat and then all of his vegetables before reaching the potatoes. After he heard me talk in class about how high intensity analysts often eat clockwise on their plate and will eat all of one thing before moving to another, the father finally understood what was going on. The potatoes were at two o'clock on the plate and the other types of food which were positioned at six o'clock and ten o'clock had to be eaten first. While it was strange to him, it made perfect sense to the son. Peace was restored to that family because of their understanding of the Windows.

When I went to see the kids' movie, *Big Hero 6* after it came out, I was pleasantly surprised to see how clearly the Windows could be seen in the different characters. The one my team and I laughed with (not at) the most was the character who was an Analyst. When the first battle was set to begin, the Analyst superhero became paralyzed because he did not know the plan, and he kept hollering, "What's the plan?" Without a known plan, it is extremely difficult for an Analyst to function to their full potential.

Understanding this linear view and way of processing has helped me so much in understanding Analysts. Before this, I had not understood that interrupting their process sent them into chaos. To all the Analysts in my life, past and present—and there are many—I apologize for the times I have done that exact thing.

I have also realized that Analysts cannot discuss a matter until they have had adequate time to process it in their head. This silence had always been unnerving to my inner Teamist, but now I just ask, "Are you in your head?" To which I often get the reply, "Yes, I am thinking through something." Once my Teamist is satisfied that our relationship is secure, I can leave them to their processing without concern. Life is much simpler.

Before coming to you to discuss something complex or serious, extreme Analysts will play out the complete conversation in their heads, even to the point of figuring out how you might respond and how they will answer in the given scenarios. Once they have completed these conversations in their heads, the dialogue sometimes becomes so real to them that they may never talk to you in person. They already have their answer, and they will swear they already talked to you if you ask.

Another lesson I have learned is that I do not have to develop the process myself. If I can give them enough information, they will go off and create a perfect process. My only problem is deciding how much information they need in order to move forward. When this happens, I ask a Producer to help. Understanding Analysts provided one of the biggest Window challenges to me for many years, but I have found that it really relieves stress in my life when I begin to work with instead of against our differences.

It's *Not* Perfectionism

While some over-developed Analysts can have a tendency toward OCD or perfectionism, it does not mean every Analyst is this way. However, many of them do not even recognize their need for perfection. They see it as "being right." Producing something that is flawed is painful for an Analyst. They are driven to do things correctly. This leads us to two other areas in the Analyst that often need softening—the "need to be right" and their inability to work in gray areas.

During my years of coaching, several Analysts have needed assistance in the area of time management because of their perfection-driven tendency. They can spend hours trying to make a graphic perfect, when most of us cannot even see its flaws. This excessive time spent puts Analysts into extreme time pressure, and paralysis sets in. They need someone to come along beside them and say, "Will anybody die if it's not perfect?" While it may be painful for them to admit that nobody will, saying this helps unstick them from their thought process and restore movement.

Have you ever seen an Analyst walk into a room and start straightening things because of the disorder? I am convinced that most of the time this is an automatic reaction to the disorder for

Analysts, and they are actually unaware they are even doing it. They see the disarray I cannot see as an Imaginist, and it unnerves them. I drive them crazy, though I do not mean to. They have a similar way of straightening when reading. Do not hand them something to read unless you can handle their automatic editing and correcting. I have learned only to pass my writing on to an Analyst at the end of a project, not during. Otherwise my creativity is stopped, though it is not their fault.

To be most proficient and effective, Analysts need order and structure in their environments. Any disorder causes them to react like a deer in headlights. This also applies to noise and chaos, not just to clutter. Often, you will find them needing to work in an isolated environment with the door closed. The only reason for this is that it helps them remain focused. However, I have also seen them so focused when walking down the hallway that they can run into someone and never even realize it. They do not ignore anyone on purpose, but they are sometimes not aware when you are near or trying to get their attention.

One of the Analysts in my life right now notices every flaw in my blouse, my makeup, or anything else I may be looking to buy. I learned a long time ago that shopping for the "perfect" Christmas tree with an Analyst is a long-term commitment and requires shaking every tree, as well as standing back and looking to see if there is anything wrong with the symmetry of the tree. I now buy artificial trees, but the Analyst visiting with me while I was putting up the tree this year spent a great deal of time fluffing the tree so that no open areas could be seen. Left to my own decorating, I would have just filled in those areas with ornaments and gone on. I became almost afraid to finish decorating it, because I was positive I would not get it "right."

Giving up the right to be right is one of the most difficult tasks a strong Analyst will ever have. People laugh when I say, "They are never wrong." However, it's true—they are seldom wrong, and if they are, it is rare for you to be able to get them to give up and admit it. They work hard to be right but not with the intention of proving you wrong. It really has nothing to do with you. For them, this is an internal need to feel good about what they have accomplished, as well as a strong internal value that says, "Do it right the first time!"

I am learning to help them achieve this in their lives. If that requires me to be wrong, so be it. I say that not with the intent of giving in to my own people pleasing tendency but of honoring who they are and what they need.

Let's talk for a minute about the problem gray areas cause Analysts. For Analysts, right is right, and wrong is wrong. Justice is paramount to them, and when injustice abounds, they are again unable to function to their highest potential. What is interesting is their lack of awareness that this is even a problem for them. I have coached two people in recent years who struggle in this area. Without realizing it, they had become extremely judgmental and intolerant of others. Their leadership was suffering because they exerted extreme pressure on those working for them, and no one could measure up to their standards. It was difficult to help them to see this, since they were being more critical of themselves than they were of anyone else. They have very high standards or expectations of themselves, as well as others.

Closing Thoughts on Analysts

There are a few general characteristics that can be seen in Analysts, and I think it helps to close out our discussion about them by reviewing them.

Attention to detail is paramount to an Analyst's dress. Everything matches, everything fits perfectly, and there are never any stains, holes, or missing buttons. Their shoes are pristine. Analyst men, in particular, attentively keep the soles of their shoes in good shape and have them resoled rather than purchasing new ones. I have often stated that Analysts look like they have come right off the cover of GQ, even when they are mowing the grass. Analysts tend to avoid bright colors. It took us a while to convince the Analyst part of my son to explore the world of color in his wardrobe. He stuck to khaki, browns, blacks, and blues for many years. My Analyst business partner was teased often (by others not me) for the matching handkerchief he always carried in the pocket of his jacket. Again, these are what I call "unconscious behaviors." They just do it.

Formal job titles are important to an Analyst so you might hear them use them in conversation or introductions. Careers that attract them are: teaching, accounting, legal work, architecture, computer programming, executive management, banking and finance, diagnostics, electronics, engineering, art restoration, technical writing, editing, politics, design, urban planning, and any data-based careers.

Analysts:
- Need eye contact—it is crucial for them to know you are listening, and a lack of eye contact tends to make them believe you are not listening
- Have difficulty functioning when things are out of order
- Are great at editing your work
- Need to feel respected

Assignment #1: If you are an Analyst, spend some time on reflecting how your thought process and need for order impacts others. Journal anything you might add to what you are already doing or change to improve understanding and clarity.

Assignment #2: If you work or live with an Analyst, how can this information change the communication and relationship between you in a positive way? What additional steps should you take?

Chapter 7
It's Hip to Be Square

When studying the Windows, one of my biggest difficulties has been learning to understand a smaller percentage of people who seem to be all over the place in their behaviors and tendencies. Upon careful observation of their scores in each Window, you will see that their graph forms almost a perfect square.

I began to realize the highest and lowest scores of all four Windows for this group were only separated by five points. I mentioned before that, when people have two scores within five points, they run back and forth between the two Windows, and it is sometimes difficult to figure out which one they live in for the majority of their time. The same is true in this situation, but here, all four Windows are within five points. These individuals are running around all of the Windows at will, which explains why I thought they were "all over the place." I was totally confused by their communication styles and behaviors, and frankly, I came away tired from trying to keep up with them.

However, there are some Squares who seemed to be what I would call naturally great communicators. These particular individuals were skilled in seeking their own clarity and in helping others reach it as well. When I looked at their graphs, I saw that they too had all four Windows within five points. The differences between these two types of Squares lead us to our next discussion.

Confused or All Together

Early in my time of working as a consultant and teaching the Windows, I was blessed to work with two individuals during the same period of time. Both were Squares; however, I, along with everyone else who worked with them, experienced an interesting phenomenon.

One lady, who was serving as a volunteer coordinator for a charity, knew that she needed to hear information from different perspectives before making a decision or before communicating effectively. She had already recognized the need to change her communication style when working with different people and instinctively knew how to do what I was trying to teach others to do. She was what I now have named an "All Together Square." She changed her own Window to meet the style of the person she was talking with. When seeking information she needed for herself, she asked enough questions of those around her to satisfy the needs of each of the four Windows. She commanded the respect of all who knew and worked with her, providing incredible relational leadership. Once she saw her own graph as the Square, she was grateful to know she was not crazy for needing to take the time for clarity.

The second Square I was working with was the total opposite. As the marketing manager for a small publishing company, she jumped around the Windows so quickly and without asking questions, that everyone working with her walked away shaking their heads and trying to figure out what had just happened in their brief interaction. Early on in our time together, I would be tired after just an hour-long coaching session with her from trying to follow her thought process and slow her down enough to help her find clarity. This was my first experience with what I now call a "Confused Square."

The confusion goes both ways—the Square is confused, and so is everyone around them. Let me explain a little more. When I talk with Confused Squares, they admit confusion because of the sometimes opposing thoughts in their own heads. This comes from not understanding the gift they have of being able to see things from all sides. Once they recognize the gift and start to use it, the confusion disappears, and a truly magnificent communicator comes forth. The confusion of others around them also goes away because the Squares have learned to acknowledge their Square natures, becoming more consistent in communication and behaviors.

Enter the Creative Procrastination Zone

Once I understood the problems my first Confused Square was facing, I was able to introduce her to John Davies' concept of the Creative Procrastination Zone, or CPZ. If you are a Square, picture a zone in the middle of the windows. Imagine yourself pulling into that zone and procrastinating before jumping to any conclusions. Ask yourself or someone in that Window, "How does this Window see this topic? What additional information do I need?" Then when you have the data from all four Windows, process it and make your decision. It worked for my Confused Square.

CPZ actually works for all of us once we really begin to understand the value of each Window and the clarity that understanding them can bring to communication. It doesn't take an inordinate amount of time or procrastination. In fact, it can become a time saver. How much time has been wasted in trying to clear misunderstandings or miscommunication? I like the old adage: "Pay me now, or pay me later." In communication I would rather pay you now and seek clarity up front than pay you later and have to clean up the mess afterward.

But let us get back to the Squares. If you work with a Square, you can help them out on occasion by practicing CPZ with them. My business partner for many years was a Square. He often reached a point where he would almost shut down when thinking through things or working on a problem. I simply would ask a few questions, sit back, and watch as he travelled through his four Windows. In about fifteen minutes, without me needing to offer any opinion or advice, he would find clarity, make a decision, and be ready to move forward.

Another Square I worked with was a city manager. He had a powerful team of other managers, many of whom were strong in their primary Windows. One by one, each would approach him about a decision the team was pondering.

The strong Producer would plead his case, and the Square easily drifted to the Producer and agreed with his conclusions. So the Producer walked out of the meeting confident that the Square would side with him in the final decision.

Next in the door came a strong Analyst, who also presented his case for a "right" decision, and the Square moved to the Analyst Window and agreed with his conclusions.

Are you beginning to see the pattern? Before long a strong Imaginist and a strong Teamist had also visited the city manager (Square) and convinced him that their view was the correct one. Imagine the surprise all of the managers felt when the Square walked into the next joint meeting without having made a definitive decision.

Upon learning about his communication style, the city manager clearly communicated to each of his other managers that he would not agree with anyone or making a final decision until all views had been heard and thought through. With this understanding, the other managers changed their expectations and methods, and no one walked around with hard feelings. In addition, decisions were actually made more quickly than before. Using CPZ helped him to avoid confusing his managers because he began waiting to respond to any one individual in a particular Window until he had heard from the other three Windows.

CPZ works for other Windows as well, but it is an essential practice for Squares in order to help them maintain their own sanity and the sanity of those around them.

It's Easy to Communicate to Squares

It is easier to communicate to Squares than to other Windows, because no matter what Window you approach them from, they can easily meet you there. Starting conversations does not take a lot of planning. However, gaining commitment from a Square requires more effort because they will waffle back and forth until they have a clear understanding of the situations from the point of view of all four Windows. Please keep in mind that it is more fun when they know they are a Square, because then you can openly talk about what their inner Teamist or Analyst need to bring greater clarity to the conversation.

I also think it is important to say something about the difference of being a relaxed Square versus a Square under pressure. A person who is a relaxed Square has achieved a balanced approach to communication. They are generally excellent leaders. Once they have a clear understanding of the Windows and of their own thought processes, any confusion that might have previously existed goes away, and they begin to use their new knowledge to provide stronger leadership, support, and guidance. Once they gain this knowledge, I do not find very many of them walking in weaknesses either. Without the knowledge, however, the biggest weakness I have found is a tendency to bounce around and an inability to clearly define their mission or purpose and where they are the happiest.

Now let's talk about someone who becomes a Square under the pressure of time. Many of those Squares are actually strong Teamists when they are relaxed, but with the added pressure of time, they feel the need to try and be all things to all people. This causes them internal stress and often reduces their effectiveness. If they become Squares under time pressure after being strong Analysts when relaxed, they may more easily walk in their strengths since the Square often is a more balanced and natural approach for them. I think this is driven by the Analyst desire to process and understand clearly situations before jumping to any conclusions. I only know of one relaxed Producer who became a Square under pressure. After being around him, it was recognizable that he was a Teamist who had moved to the Producer window early in his life as a form of survival from hurt.

Squares are not very common, and other than mentioning the closeness of their scores, John Davies did not include any data on them in his original research. Because Squares are so rare, it has taken me twenty-plus years to spend the amount of time with them necessary to draw reliable conclusions.

Don't Change to Become a Square

When teaching this material, I run into many people who think their goal should be to change to become a Square. I do not believe that is the optimum solution. I believe we are all created to be who we are. Later, we will discuss our differences a little more. For now, be willing to recognize that it is not about changing who you are but about learning to shift your style of communication for short periods of time in order to bring clarity when communicating with others. Do not give up the way you view any given situation—just seek to understand those around you and find clarity in your conversations. Additionally, you should be willing to help the other person do the same with your viewpoint.

I believe that we can learn to walk in the Square's ability to Window hop without striving to become a Square ourselves. Discernment, wisdom, and grace abound, allowing a free flow of exchange and supernatural understanding. Don't drive yourself to become something you were not created to be. Just be who you are, and practice Window hopping for clarity.

Assignment #1: If you are a Square (or very close to being one), spend some time reflecting on what you have learned about yourself. How has that impacted your communication with others' to date?

Assignment #2: If you work or live with a Square, how can this information enhance your communication with them?

Chapter 8
It's Not About "Right or Wrong" but About Respecting Differences

I have often been baffled as to why we feel the need to prove ourselves "right" and others "wrong" in our communication. Communication should be less about right and wrong, and more about gaining clarity and understanding. No one has all the answers to everything. We need each other to bounce thoughts around with, bringing the best understanding of any given situation.

In his book, *The Fifth Discipline: The Art & Practice of The Learning Organization*, Peter M. Senge talked about the power of "dialogue." In fact one of the five disciplines he teaches on is team learning. He said, "Team learning starts with dialogue, the capacity of members of a team to suspend assumptions and enter into genuine thinking together." Using the Windows to try and bring clarity is a great example of this.

For many years, I have said that the greatest power the Windows provide us with is a way to lessen our judgmental attitudes and to walk in love toward those who think and speak differently than us, but the Windows are also a great tool for building a more effective team.

Breaking the Cycle of Laying Blame

I am not a psychologist. However, as an executive coach specializing in communication and leadership, I constantly try to understand our need to find someone to blame for misunderstandings. When we begin to grasp the differences in communication styles, it is so freeing to accept that the intentions behind words, actions, or reactions are not always what I perceive them to be. I am filtering everything through my own filters, which might be polar opposite to the filters of the person I am communicating with.

With that in mind, how can one person be right and another be wrong? Our perspectives are just different. One of the most powerful quotes I have heard recently came from Susan Scott's book, *Fierce Conversations: Achieving Success at Work and in Life One Conversation at a Time.* She says, "In any given situation, the person who can most accurately describe reality without laying blame will emerge as the leader, whether designated or not."

We live in a society of "he said," "she said," and "they said" which catapults us into a faultfinding frenzy that provokes all of us to take defensive postures in which nothing is easily resolved.

We need to learn to seek clarity not blame.

Understanding Our Differences Brings Clarity

When we are willing to step back into the middle of a conversation and ask, "What do you mean?" or say, "I'm not sure I understand what you are saying," we open the door for greater clarity and reduce the chance of our differences causing misunderstanding. Understanding the differences in meanings of words and seeking clarity can be great tools—a truth that I have seen over and over again in coaching times or general conversations. Often our coaching involves resolving conflict. When you find yourself in those types of situations, try asking every member in the conversation to define a particular word or to clarify their meanings about something. This can resolve conflict quicker than anything else. Try using the phrase, "I know what [this word] means to me. What does it mean to you?" And then sit back and watch the communication differences unfold.

Sometimes it is not just about the definitions of words but about understanding the underlying influence of time. When listening through the present time frame of the Producer, urgency becomes a defining factor. This can bring confusion to the past time frame of the Teamist, who is more interested in building the relationship than in worrying about getting something done quickly. Taking the time up front to question possible differences in the Producer and Teamist's thought processes or meanings can save enormous amounts of time on the back side of a conversation, especially since those differences might have led to misunderstandings.

Just today, as I was taking some much-needed time away from work to concentrate on writing, I received a text message from someone encouraging me to go for long walks in between my times of writing. Walking invigorates her, but it tires me out. If I went walking, I would have to come back and go to bed, not continue writing.

The difference between the two of us could have been a source of misunderstanding. However, I know our differences, so I just chalked it up to that fact that we are different and that was okay. My people pleaser no longer has to comply with her suggestion, allowing me to say thanks for the suggestion and move on. Nothing was right or wrong about either of our approaches—they were just different.

Another example of the impact of understanding our differences came up a coaching session recently. When we are coaching someone, we often have to challenge them to realize that what they think or believe about an action is not always perceived by another person in the same way. In this case, we suggest that our client develop a habit of communicating on a frequent basis with the person he reports to directly. His initial perception was that this was brown-nosing or bragging about himself. We asked him to consider that his supervisor saw it as being open and willing to keep him informed as to what was happening where our client was located—a considerable distance from the supervisor. We proposed that communicating frequently was providing information, not seeking recognition, and would avoid future situations of the supervisor finding things out after the fact or from other people, or—in the worst case scenario—making an incorrect assumption about what is happening because he had too little information. It took a little influence to get our client to see the differences and agree to communicate on a more frequent basis, not only in a crisis.

How often we should communicate, how we should communicate, and what we should communicate are all areas in which people may show differences in preference, style, and views of time. Making incorrect assumptions about a co-worker or friend's answers to these questions can result in confusion, misunderstandings, or relationship issues.

We Need Our Differences to See the Whole Picture

If we rely only on our own perceptions, we do not always know everything, nor do we have a complete understanding of what is happening. Unless we are blessed to be Squares, our perception processes generally filter out something that would give us complete understanding if we knew it. Going forward, I challenge you to remember this and to find a friend or co-worker who is strong in the Window that you are weak in. Bounce your thoughts around with that person, and it just might give you an opportunity to see the whole picture.

In our organization we practice this technique frequently in coaching, and especially in coaching teams. We work to get our clients to see various situations through the perception processes of the different Windows. To help them understand their inability to do this on their own, we have adopted a teaching strategy from leadership coach and consultant Susan Scott. We recommend her books to all of our clients, and she has profoundly impacted many of us.

In this object lesson, we ask them to hold a multi-colored beach ball, assigning a particular color to each person. One person will be blue, another red, another green, etc. Then they are asked to describe their environment in terms of that color. The blue person will see everything in blue—a blue chair, blue desk, blue paper, blue stapler. The red person, on the other hand, will view everything as red. Through the exercise, participants realize that they filter experiences through their Window in the same way that they filtered their surroundings through their color. It is amazing how a simple visual can help bring clarity.

Finding the truth in any given situation requires understanding our differences and a willingness to seek clarity. The ultimate solution or answer is more often than not a combination of everyone's points of view.

How many times have you heard the phrase, "Birds of a feather flock together"? When discussing difficult matters, we have a tendency to reach out only to those we think will agree with us. Life is easier that way. However, next time, try seeking out those you know who might disagree with you. They may have a piece of information about the situation that you are missing or cannot see. Learning that information can bring great clarity and resolution.

Let's Embrace Our Weaknesses

How many of you carry around a big stick and frequently use it to beat yourself up about one of your weaknesses? I was guilty of that for many years. Learning to put the stick down permanently is not easy, but it has great benefits, particularly in terms of communication. Instead of beating myself up over weaknesses today, I choose to look to those around me who have strengths I do not in order to help me overcome my weaknesses. I do not use my weakness as an excuse to say, "That's just the way I am."

Several people in my life have a tendency to stay in their heads too much or to overthink things to the point of sheer frustration or stress. Rather than criticize them, I attempt to use my own strength of exploring possibilities to get them out of their heads and help them engage in dialogue to bring them to their own clarity. These are the same people I ask to help me overcome my own weakness of not always seeing distinctions or details. Their ability to see things I might be missing can save me a lot of anguish and time.

Our team at ILD practices this technique with each other and in our team meetings. We want to work in our own areas of strength and minimize any wasted time because of our weaknesses. However, if there is a weakness we can fix, then we help each other do that. We call out each other's weaknesses in love, and as a result, our team is always growing and becoming better.

Assignment #1: Look at these three questions:
- How often should we communicate?
- How should we communicate?
- What should we communicate?

Determine your communication styles, preferences, and time frames for each question. Then identify at least two other people with whom you need to communicate regularly, and analyze how their communication styles, preferences, and time frames different from yours. Have these differences caused issues for you in the past? If so, what can you do differently about these things now? If you are not sure, make an effort to sit down with the other person and work through your differences to gain clarity.

Assignment #2: Challenge a group of people you spend time with on a regular basis to practice this technique of hearing all points of view on a topic. Pay special attention to those who are different than you in order to bring greater clarity and understanding.

What happened as result of this exercise? Was it hard for some to engage? How did sticking it out make a difference?

Assignment #3: What communication weaknesses would you benefit from fixing if you can, or embracing if you cannot by finding someone to cover for you in that area? How could using this model to deal with your weaknesses benefit you going forward?

Chapter 9
The Combinations of Styles Are Most Challenging

When I first teach people about the Windows, I place most of the emphasis on the four quadrants of Producer, Imaginist, Teamist, and Analyst. For the most part, we hear first out of our strongest Window, so learning about those four quadrants will help you learn to recognize style differences between them. However, very few people operate purely out of one Window. Most of us have two or even three Windows we are very comfortable operating out of, so when we read about the pure Windows, we have difficulty seeing ourselves. That is why John Davies went to the effort of developing names and descriptions for the six possible combinations of the Windows.

The combinations are as follows:

Producer & Imaginist = Speculator
Producer & Teamist = Accumulator
Producer & Analyst = Investigator
Imaginist & Teamist = Integrator
Imaginist & Analyst = Conceiver
Teamist & Analyst = Organizer

The names remain the same, no matter which Window has a higher intensity. If the point spread between two of your Windows is 0-9, we recommend you read the appropriate combination description, but becoming familiar with the combination is most important when the point spread is only 0-5. Any time a person's highest Window is ten points higher than the other three, they tend to view everything through only one Window.

Why Pay Attention to the Numbers?

The goal has always been to use the Windows to reduce frustration and gain clarity, so paying attention to the numbers becomes vitally important when dealing with combination Windows. When two people have the same two highest Windows, it is easy to assume they view life the same way. However, this is not always true. A

Teamist/Producer is slightly different than a Producer/Teamist, and the numbers help explain why. Someone with a Teamist score of 28 and a Producer score of 25 will filter experiences through his Teamist Window most often. On the other hand, someone with a Producer score of 28 and a Teamist score of 25 will filter experiences through her Producer Window most often. The slight flip-flop in their scores will affect how they behave and communicate.

For example, I worked with one couple that were in the same two Windows but always had opposite points of view from each other. He was an Analyst/Imaginist, and she was an Imaginist/Analyst. Getting in the same Window at the same time often proved challenging for them, so seeing the problem on paper and beginning to work on it made a huge difference in their marriage and work life.

It is not uncommon to see opposites marry, even in the combinations. My son, the Imaginist/Analyst (Conceiver) married a Producer/Teamist (Accumulator). They are perfect for each other and are an example to me of working in their strengths and covering each other's weaknesses.

As you continue to grow in your understanding of how to use the Windows in your everyday life, pay attention to the numbers and the subtle differences they can make in relating to each other. Sometimes the differences are quite obvious—just remember we are walking in love and avoiding judgment of our differences.

The Combinations

Let's take a brief look at the major indicators of each combination. We will not go as deep into these as we did with our four main Windows, but this should help you recognize each combination in everyday life.

SPECULATORS

Speculators are a combination of the Producer (present) Window and the Imaginist (future) Window. This combination is one of the rarest ones and is known for being able to see opportunity in every experience. They see the risk versus results and are able to create time for imagined ideas before immediately moving on to focus on the present actions needed to turn a dream into a tangible commodity. Speculators have been credited with creating such things as pet rocks, hula hoops, and McDonald's hamburgers.

In my years of working with Speculators, I have found that many of them have been accused of having ADHD. The extremity of their difficulties in paying attention depends on whether the Producer or the Imaginist is higher. However, they are also touted as being entrepreneurs, "self-made" successes, tycoons, and giants of industry. They are skilled at balancing chance and necessity, and their ability to see hidden or unique values in business often cause others to see them as antagonists or trouble makers or to think that they do not commit enough time for people. Speculators are not long-range planners or thinkers but rather medium-range gamblers.

Behaviorally, they tend to be high energy and sometimes negative. In conversation, they avoid being overly specific and sometimes ask "stupid-smart" questions, They enjoy playing devil's advocate and often propose opposing ideas or arguments, constantly contradicting themselves without blame. They thrive on conflict, confusion, and ambiguity.

Speculators use phrases like:
- "Don't worry about tomorrow . . ."
- "What's our timing . . . ?"
- "Make it happen . . ."
- "Let's go for it . . ."
- "Let's not sit and think . . ."
- "When is it needed . . . ?"

The subtle differences between the numbers will change their focus slightly. It is impossible to describe every difference here but a few examples are as follows. If the Imaginist is higher than the Producer, the Speculator is more likely to be ADHD and to use a lot of intuition in making decisions. If the Producer is higher than the Imaginist, the Speculator will react quickly, ignoring intuition and risking failure because thinking too long is a waste of time.

ACCUMULATORS

Accumulators are a combination of the Producer (present) Window and the Teamist (past) Window. They are extremely adept at sorting through assignments quickly, making decisions, assigning people to tasks, and creating a team. They never work for nothing and are not motivated by praise or letters of recommendation. They prefer material items such as rings, prizes (they love contests), and, if their Teamist score is higher, peer recognition.

Accumulators value time for people and tangible results. In short, they work hard with, for, and through people to obtain solid results for their efforts. They excel in concrete accomplishments and love careers in production management, sales, sports, service industries, and medicine. They are often labeled as movers and shakers, action takers, and hasty decision-makers. They like to share their experiences and prefer environments alive with people and activity. They vacillate from being called "good old boy" or "real friend" one minute to being perceived as a "sledge-hammer," "shyster," or "going for the throat" the next minute.

They work hard and play hard and find themselves colored with busyness even in relaxation. They tend to be warm and personable with friends and family, but they are abrupt and assertive with others.

Accumulators speak passionately, talk fast, and use both urgent expressions and personal appeals.

Some of their favorite expressions include:
- "Do me a favor."
- "You're holding me up."
- "I've got to run."
- "Let me show you."

- "I'm too busy right now."
- "Hey, good buddy."

INVESTIGATORS

Investigators are a combination of the Producer (present) Window and the Analyst (balance of past, present, and future) Window. People with the acquired dominance of this very common combination are adept at producing "bottom-line results" and are perceived by others as "achievers." They have a tendency to value quantified accomplishment and to devalue sentimental purposes in doing anything.

Over 75 percent of those in middle management have a strong propensity for this Window's combination and exemplify the "plan your work and work your plan" philosophy. They write books on time management principles and can lose patience with those who do not follow the rules. They are masters at creating external environmental change; however, they may resist the effort to create internal value changes.

They strive for high standards themselves and hold others to the same standards. They are sometimes accused of caring too much about numbers. Investigators exhibit steady and responsible work habits and high levels of self-discipline. They become skilled policy-makers.

Investigators communicate in a "cut-and-dried" style of speaking, prefer moving from point to point, and place a high value on documented communications. Providing Investigators with agendas before meetings is a must so that they can be thoroughly prepared. They use their well-developed language abilities to speak in precise terms, logical patterns, and measured delivery.

Some of their favorite phrases include:
- "The point I am trying to make is . . ."
- "My studies reveal . . ."
- "The only logical thing is . . ."
- "Let's sleep on it . . ."

- "Can you substantiate your . . . ?"
- "Expert opinion says . . ."
- "The best sequence of action is . . ."

Their acute and focused time perceptions translate into linear or behaviors in work and play. They say the "right" things, wear the "right" things, and participate in the "right" activities. They exhibit very polarized thinking through their communications, which reveal extreme orientations of right and wrong, good and bad, positive and negative, brilliant and dumb judgments. They do not deal well with gray areas.

Finally, Investigators value scheduled events, planned activities— including vacations—and a balance to fun and work.

INTEGRATORS

Integrators are a combination of the Imaginist (future) Window and the Teamist (past) Window. They are adept at unifying and creating wholes out of fragmented or diverse situations. This combination is characterized by an almost completely open, fluid, and unstructured approach to business and personal affairs.

The higher their Imaginist score is, the greater their need is to understand "why" about everything. They have a natural curiosity which causes them to ask lots of questions, driving others insane. They have little interest in concrete reality or down-to-earth activities, showing greater interest in kicking ideas around and discussing them with others. Integrators usually possess a powerful persuasive ability to convince others to join them in something.

Integrators are voracious readers of a broad range of topics, but they may not finish reading many of the books they start. They suffer from mental paradigm shifts (such as going from being fully engaged with others to suddenly isolating themselves by retreating into a world of thought), which confuse those around them and may make them appear as though they lack rhyme or reason. They can be deeply emotional and are sometimes accused of "ballooning" things out of proportion in their communication.

Some of their favorite sayings are:
- "There's more than meets the eye . . ."
- "Jumping ahead, we can . . ."
- "In a more holistic sense . . ."
- "Can you feel the intensity of . . . ?"
- "My interpretation is . . ."
- "Imagine how they feel . . ."

Integrators like to keep all their options open and may avoid commitment as a result. They can be seen as scatter-brained, and they enjoy working in gray areas. They are strong "internalizers," taking things personally and then avoiding confrontation by escaping into their mind's world of possibilities.

They determine the duration of their time involvement by the depth and novelty of the experience or by the potential positive impact on other people, whole departments, or entire societies. Overall, the determining factors in setting their priorities depend on the level of potential for discovery or on the relational component.

CONCEIVERS

The Conceiver is a combination of the Imaginist (future) Window and the Analyst (balance of past, present, and future) Window. They excel in creating and devote their time to evolutionary growth or alternative methods for progress. They combine the diffused, exploratory time perception of the Imaginist with the paradoxical focused on linear details of an Analyst—both important elements for creating something.

They are intellectually tough, individualistic, and highly defensive of their creations or ideas. Conceivers are adept at asking abstract questions that turn generalities into precise, concentrated elements ready for additional development. They can be perceived as unwilling to compromise or adapt.

They can also excel in articulation, moving back and forth from their ability to speak in universal terms to becoming ultra-precise in their exacting explanations. They can spend an inordinate amount of time in their heads over-rationalizing or dissecting data. One Conceiver I know frequently gets stuck in his head while trying to decide between the two opposing thought processes of his Analyst and Imaginist. His dilemma becomes increasingly obvious to those around him by his isolation and lack of communication. "Your Imaginist is warring with your Analyst," I'll tell him, and he will reply, "How did you guess?"

Some of their favorite phrases are:
- "Intuitively, I saw . . ."
- "More research is needed . . ."
- "Other possibilities include . . ."
- "Building on the work of . . ."
- "Hypothetically speaking . . ."
- "My measurements show . . ."
- "From another point of view . . ."

They are naturally inventive, creative, and research-driven. Their work environments can be labeled as "disorganized order." They value time—personal time, quiet time, and experiential time—for exploring their diverse perspectives before providing detailed direction for change. They tend to have smaller, closed circles of colleagues, peers, or professional interest groups that are focused on highly specialized interests. They may not be interested in leading, but they love being the pathfinders.

ORGANIZERS

The Organizer combines the Teamist (past) Window with the Analyst (balance of past, present, and future) Window. They are adept at pulling people together to accomplish planned goals. They value traditional practices, proven methods, guaranteed results, and daily routines.

Organizers are often said to be serious thinkers, highly moralistic, and eminently trustworthy. They are motivated by teamwork strategies and accomplishments, and they love receiving recognition for those accomplishments. They can coordinate anything from the smallest operation to a major, organization-wide function for companies, cities, or governments.

They are usually very patient people and like taking time to "go over it one more time." They can also be extremely stubborn, digging in their heels and refusing to move until they are convinced the right outcome will result from moving or changing.

Organizers suffer a "head-heart" dilemma when making decisions related to time. It is hard for them to ignore their gut feelings that come as a result of past lessons learned when they also see the sound logic for a proposed action. They tend to make correct decisions, but they can be paralyzed for a time by their desire to know more or think about it. As leaders they are strong proponents of following the chain of command and appreciate others going through them to get to any of their staff.

Like Investigators, you find many of Organizers in middle management in organizations because of their keen ability to find the best path through complex, disorganized, or chaotic situations.

They usually display a large vocabulary and are adept in linguistic clarity, verbal consistency, and memorization of quotes.

Favorite sayings of the Organizer include:
- "My people suggest . . ."
- "We need a meeting to decide . . ."
- "Who's at fault . . . ?"
- "Let's review the situation . . ."
- "Our contingency plan is . . ."
- "According to [name] . . ."
- "Past experience tells me . . ."
- "I believe we need to clarify . . ."

They can bring high levels of concentration to bear upon sensitive policy or people issues. They often behave as if they have exclusive insights into the "heart of the matter." Organizers have a need to be right.

Organizers place high value on developing things that will have a long-term, repeated usage or symbolic significance.

Assignment #1: Do you know your own combination? How does this understanding bring greater clarity to your own communication needs and your reactions to others?

Assignment #2: Where have you seen subtle changes in people that you know as a result of their combination communication styles? Does it bring greater clarity? What can you do going forward with this knowledge?

Chapter 10
Time Is the Key

I believe John Davies' use of time as the qualifier to distinguish each communication style was quite brilliant. It makes the Windows so easy to remember and brings greater clarity when you begin to apply the time frame to responses and behaviors. Again, the behavior tendencies of any Window are not intended to become an excuse but to provide a place of understanding. As you begin to practice identifying the styles of communication yourself, looking at each situation through the lens of time can be very helpful.

Understanding the Impact of Time on Each Window Pane

Let's take a look at each Window again in order to apply this principle of time and see what happens. First, I would like to discuss each Window in terms of its time perception and then describe some examples of how this affects day-to-day interactions.

PRODUCERS

The focused perception of Producers causes them to see time as fast-paced. Time is running out, and there is never enough of it. Add to that their discontinuous perception which causes them to see each event separately without trying to connect how time will flow to their benefit. They live and think in a world of the present, or now. This results in a task-focused individual running around like a bull in a china shop, trying to get things done and viewing everyone and everything else as getting in their way. They quickly lose sight of past events, even those as recent as five minutes ago, and they don't care about tomorrow, or even this afternoon. It's all about what they have to do now. This creates a never-ending urgency in them to keep things moving and can also drive their passion and bring them to intense levels of impatience.

IMAGINISTS

The diffused perception of Imaginists causes them to see time as expansive. There is plenty of it, and it is something to be enjoyed. The addition of their discontinuous perception causes them to lose sight of what has just happened and skip merrily into tomorrow and all of its possibilities. They live and think in a world of the future, or tomorrow. What you get as a result is a laid back, fun-loving individual, who doesn't seem to have a care in the world or an urgency to do anything. John Davies called them navel watchers and masters at procrastination. I have always added that they make procrastination into an art. They can spend hours talking about various subjects or myriad of ideas, keeping everyone in the room laughing, and not accomplishing anything of importance. They usually are the ones to drive others to impatience.

TEAMISTS

The diffused perception of the Teamists causes them, like the Imaginists, to see time as expansive, plenteous, and something to be enjoyed. Their continuous perception causes them to see everything as connected to something else that happened in their past, and they love reminiscing about those events or stories. They live and think in a world of the past, or yesterday. They are filled with stories of past relationships and experiences, making them avid storytellers. They always have time to talk and share their experiences. They are easily put off by those who aren't willing to engage in casual conversation before delving into the necessary. Speed or urgency makes them uncomfortable and less trusting.

ANALYSTS

The focused perception of the Analyst causes them, like the Producers, to see time as fast-paced. Time is running out, and there is never enough time to be sure everything they are doing is correct. Their continuous perception causes them to connect in sequential order the past events that led up to where you are currently before moving ahead. They live and think in a world of the past, which is chronologically connected to the present, which gives you future, risk-free options when analyzed (balance of past, present, and future). They must have time to assess all three time frames, or they become unable to move, like a deer in headlights. They can appear stuck at times and may need help re-ordering their thoughts to get back on track.

Now you have a baseline to use when working with other Windows to help you filter your perceptions of what they are saying or doing through their filter of time. Ideally, you will gain greater clarity as a result. They aren't behaving the way they do to aggravate you—they are actually just processing the events through their own time perceptions, which may or may not match yours.

Time Pressure, *Not* Always Stress

The fact that time pressure is not always equivalent to stress is sometimes a difficult concept for people to grasp. It seems natural to equate pressure to stress. However, only one Window actually does that—the Analyst, because time is their stress factor. There is never enough time for them to be adequately sure of the correctness of what they are working on or wanting to say.

So let's see if we can get to a place of understanding our time pressure profiles versus our relaxed time profiles. Our relaxed profiles are our default perceptions, which we operate under when time is not an issue. Another way of describing this is how we behave when no one is looking. One of my coaches, a very strong Producer is a good example of this. Even when no one else is around, he is still focused on getting things done and always has a list a mile long. Believe me he can get things done. I often wonder if he stops to sleep. It is hard to get him to stop long enough to listen during a coaches meeting or to get through a meeting without him experiencing phone call interruptions or needing to leave in a hurry for another meeting. His leg will be bouncing a mile a minute the whole time, but that's just who he is.

Time pressure, on the other hand, causes us to think that how we would normally operate is not working, so we must adapt. Some of us just intensify our current Windows, while others of us make dramatic switches to another Window. That Window becomes our adaptive behavior or thinking style for the duration of the time pressure. This can sometimes easily be seen in the difference between the way a person acts at home or in the office. However, time pressure can occur anywhere, and how we adapt changes with every situation because we are adapting to our environment and the associated time pressure. So do not get hung-up on a person's time pressure scores or graph, because as soon as you think you have it figured it out and begin to expect it, it can change.

Let us spend some time now looking at stress.

Stress is defined as the mind and body's adaptation to change. Stress for a Producer is called "situational" because it occurs when the Producer deems the current situation out of control. This causes them to react like a stick of dynamite. They blow up, rant, rave, and become a dictator, pushing others out of the way to bring back control. Then, as soon as the situation is handled, they will waltz out the door, absolutely calm. They can return five minutes later ready to go to lunch and totally oblivious to the havoc they caused five minutes earlier. This situation caused by stress is completely different from one of intensified time pressure in which Producers are in an exasperated state of movement from trying to accomplish a task.

Stress to an Imaginist is brought on by the "anticipation" of something, which might or might not happen. They begin hypothesizing all the possibilities in their head. This causes them to retreat into what I call a cave, or into their thoughts, as they completely disconnect from everything and everyone around them. If left alone, their stress can build from tiny speck to a giant hairball of consequences. You may see them as being indifferent in this situation. This is why I suggest you ask them, "What are you seeing?" This will allow them to open the cave door and let you into their thoughts. Sometimes, just verbalizing their thoughts out loud will reduce their stress; other times, you may need to help them focus on their options.

To a Teamist, stress is caused by "disharmony." They have difficulty functioning beyond their emotions or feelings if they sense someone is upset with them, if they are upset with someone, or if there is tension in a room they enter. This stress is intensified by the fact that, because of their continuous view, they won't be able to tell whether they brought the disharmony with them or whether it was already there when they arrived. They become uber-sensitive, taking everything around them personally, whether it was intended that way or not. It may take extra time for Teamists to get to a reactive stage, because they will overlook, make excuses for what's going on, and pretend everything is okay. However, there will be a breaking point when they come out of the corner with their elephant memory list intact and verbally attack, reminding everyone involved of everything that has been done and said in regard to a certain situation. Sometimes this list goes as far back as six months. If they are walking in weakness, they may stuff the new memories away for later use once the onslaught of verbiage has ceased. It takes time and effort to help them work through the memories and clear the slate. Your assistance will be most needed up front to help them become willing to verbalize what they are feeling before it reaches the boiling point.

To the Analyst, as we already mentioned, stress is time pressure. They are always "under the time gun," analyzing for perfection because they abhor being wrong. Similar to the Imaginist, they enter the cave and shut down as the stress is building, but they enter this cave in order to get their ducks in a row. Beware that when their ducks are ordered, they will emerge from their cave and behave much like the Producer, only they will have justification for their decision and will likely be unwilling to discuss anything further. They are right, the decision has been made, and that is it.

It Is Worth Your Time to See if It Works for You

I feel like singing, "What a difference it has made in my life!" I no longer cringe at the thought of making someone upset or of getting upset myself because of someone else's words or actions. I welcome different communication styles, different perceptions, and different behaviors as an opportunity for me to learn, grow, and gain clarity.

You have my testimony. Now here are some testimonials we have received over years of teaching this material:

"I was first exposed to the Time Communication Model when I joined the Bowater, Inc. leadership team in Catawba, South Carolina. The thing that impressed me most was that . . . employees were still using the Model to guide their interactions and communications several years after Rebecca had introduced it there.

Since that time I have used the Model in several developmental and training programs, and find that it continues to add value when used as a stand-alone or adjunct tool for helping individuals and/or teams communicate more effectively. I find it particularly effective in helping people understand the impact of time pressure and conflict situations. I can recommend it without reservation."

Kenny Sawyer
Sr. Vice President, HR & Communications
Verso Corporation

"Communication is the key to everything—life in general, interpersonal relationships of every kind, and effectiveness in our chosen vocation. Rebecca Rhodes' new book provides both insights guaranteed to demystify the art of communication and practical steps to enhance our competencies as communicators. I highly recommend it!"

Phil Needham
Retired Commissioner
Salvation Army Southern Territory

"I was all over the place when it came to time management. Once I understood that my top value is relationship, I was able to change my priorities for the better, as well as ensure I am able to meet deadlines without last-minute stress."

R.H.
General Manager
Community Coop

"Thank you for introducing me to this life changing tool. I now understand that communication is born in the heart, mind, and soul. Knowledge and desire to be an effective communicator saved my marriage, changed my perspective on life, and gave me a new love for people as I implemented the tools. I am a new and improved version of my inner self. Read the book, and be reborn!"

Rhonda Jane Catha-Kramer
Life Coach

"Thank you so much for what you brought us at Cabo. It truly was enlightening and freeing. I feel as though I got a clearer picture of myself. Keep rocking it!"

Tai Ann McClendon

"Spending time with Rebecca and her team on the Time and Communication Model has been a great experience. My participation with the Model has led to more effective communication with my colleagues. Learning the differences in how people respond to situations based on their natural tendencies [and] knowing your own style and recognizing the styles of others greatly increases productivity and fosters a positive culture. Using the tools allows one to learn 'behaviors' that move you and your team toward greater production without as many negative consequences. Well worth the investment of our resources!"

Jeff Meadows
Senior Development Officer
Charlotte Housing Authority, NC

"I'm not sure where to begin. [For] John as a pilot (Analyst) and me as a creative (Teamist), [being] married has been quite the challenge. When I began to study and coach the materials from ILD, I had no idea that the information was going to transform my communication with John. All the little things that seemed to be a constant challenge in communication began to be no issue. It was so gradual that one day John just asked if I was in counseling. Needless to say, I started looking at all the other Windows and realized the 'magic' involved in a great way to communicate.

I'm so thankful to be heard and to hear others from their Window. Thank you, Rebecca. I'm grateful."

Mintie Dudley

"[The] 'Welcome to My Windows' communication class has given me a wealth of confidence in dealing with teammates and . . . all interpersonal relationships. I use the handouts at least once a week."

John Stanley

"[Earlier in my career], I was the continuous improvement facilitator and shipping supervisor and reported to the operations manager. We were in a meeting with the production manager and the production planner. The operations manager asked me to find out something very simple and report back to him. . . . In the meeting the next morning, I told him what I found. About two days later, he asked me again, and I told him that I had already told him, and the production manager and production planner agreed that I had. A couple of days later, he and I got into a heated argument about the subject; he insisted that I needed to give him the information, and [I insisted] that I had already answered him.

"I had mentioned this to Rebecca before, and she [had] reminded me that he was a high Analyst and needed details and numbers. At the time I dismissed it because it seemed so simple to me. After the argument I contacted Rebecca again, and she insisted that I write it down and include dates, times, and numbers where possible. Not having any bright ideas myself, I did as instructed. . . . To my surprise after submitting this, he thanked me, and that was the end of the incident. I have worked for [another] manager [who] is also a high Analyst for approximately the past twenty years, and I have not had those types of issues since. Thank you, Rebecca!"

Otis R. Wilson
HR Manager
Duff Norton

"I have known Rebecca for many years. She lives what she communicates. Her teachings using the Time Communication Model have brought to my life the enlightenment of the pursuit of all our lives . . . the quest of understanding people. That mainly includes me. So thankful for all I learned!"

Pastor Mike Littlejohn

"I can say without hesitation that your training has had a positive impact on our co-workers and our ability to better serve our customers, the citizenry."

Jo Atwater
HR Director
City of Concord, NC

Take Time to Learn about Yourself and Apply to Others

Now we are ready to begin our journey of putting what we have learned into practical use. First, take time to understand yourself.

Assignment #1: Explore your answers to the following questions:
- What is the most significant thing I have learned about myself from this material that I can use to keep growing?
- How can I adapt my communication style to influence understanding and reduce frustration in my interactions with other Windows?
- What have I learned about my weaknesses that I can fix? What can't I fix?
- What is the most significant thing I have learned that will help me work with others differently?
- How can I use this in my daily life?

Assignment #2: Begin to apply what you have learned from the Windows material at least once daily. Journal or take notes on the results.

About the Author

Rebecca M. Rhodes is an executive leadership coach/trainer, and the founder and president of the Institute of Leadership Development (ILD). With more than three decades of professional coaching and training experience, Rebecca has taught communication, time management, and other leadership skills to thousands of individuals and organizations. Since ILD's origin in 1989, Rebecca and her team have used the Time Communication Model to help groups such as government agencies, law firms, hospitals, corporations, non-profit agencies, churches, and universities improve communication and change organizational cultures.

In addition to training other coaches, Rebecca is an established facilitator in change management, conflict resolution, and culture change. Having personally experienced the life-changing impact of the material she teaches, she is passionate about helping people improve communication and become more effective relational leaders in all walks of life. She does her best to "walk the talk" as she serves her clients and staff.

Rebecca is currently on the board of directors for a non-profit agency near her home in South Carolina. When not working or spending time at home with her husband, she also loves jamming on her keyboard, doing crafts with her young granddaughter, and sharing stories around the fire pit with her extended family.

Made in the USA
Monee, IL
04 May 2023

33017628R00080